SECT, CULT, AND CHURCH IN ALBERTA

SOCIAL CREDIT IN ALBERTA

ITS BACKGROUND AND DEVELOPMENT

A series of studies sponsored by the Canadian Social Science Research Council, directed and edited by S. D. Clark. The series is now complete.

Sect, Cult and Church in Alberta

BY W. E. MANN

UNIVERSITY OF TORONTO PRESS

Copyright, Canada, 1955
by University of Toronto Press
Toronto and Buffalo

Reprinted 1962, 1972
Printed in Canada
ISBN 0-8020-5036-0 (cloth)
ISBN 0-8020-6140-0 (paper)
LC 56-2838

TO
CANON MORLAND P. LAMB, D.D.
RECTOR OF ST. CUTHBERT'S CHURCH, LEASIDE, ONTARIO
1910–1954

Foreword

As THE SIXTH in a series sponsored by the Canadian Social Science Research Council relating to the background and development of the Social Credit movement in Alberta, it is the purpose of this study by Dr. W. E. Mann to indicate the nature of those religious conditions in the province of Alberta out of which the Social Credit movement grew. In doing this, the study calls attention to an aspect of the development of the western Canadian community which has been peculiarly neglected. Thus in their *Pioneering in the Prairie Provinces*, a study of the social side of the settlement process, Dawson and Younge could devote two chapters to an analysis of religious organization in western Canada without once mentioning the existence of the kind of religious groups which Dr. Mann writes about.[1] Other studies of the western Canadian community have similarly paid little attention to the growth of new forms of religious organization outside the traditional churches.

This curious neglect may be accounted for in part at least by what might be called the secular bias of early observers of the western Canadian community. Though there was a large literature on American evangelical religious movements, it did not seem possible to believe that rationally minded people in the twentieth century (and particularly such rationally minded people as those in western Canada!) could behave like the early settlers of upper New York State, western Pennsylvania, Kentucky, or Upper Canada who had gathered together by the thousands in camp or other kinds of religious meetings. The growth in western Canada of strong farmer political and co-operative movements (and the decline in strength of the traditional churches) appeared to demonstrate the predominantly rational outlook of the rural population, and if there were still as late as 1930 small pockets of people such as Mennonites, Doukhobors, Mormons, and German and French Catholics who sought to maintain certain cherished ethnic-spiritual values, strong secular forces, it

[1]C. A. Dawson and Eva R. Younge, *Pioneering in the Prairie Provinces: The Social Side of the Settlement Process* (Toronto, 1940), chaps. XI, XII.

vii

seemed, were steadily breaking down their isolation[2] and the time was not far distant when all the people of western Canada would come to share in the secular values characteristic of twentieth-century urban-industrial society.

Certainly, in 1930, all the evidence did point to a marked falling off in the support of the traditional churches in the rural communities of western Canada. Much of Saskatchewan and Alberta had been settled in the years 1900–13, and, though there were among the first settlers of these provinces many who had no religious faith, most brought with them a strong religious heritage. Early historical records reveal how valiant were the efforts to establish in the new pioneer settlements some sort of church services. These efforts, however, largely failed. While churches multiplied in numbers in the small towns, and fierce competition led to efforts to win the support of all sections of the population through the development of Sunday schools, young people's societies, women's organizations, and the like, rural communities at best were offered only a Sunday service which had little social appeal. The result was that in a great number of western rural communities, by 1925, scarcely a single person ever went to church. Religious values among a large section of the population had come to have practically no meaning.

In the meantime, there had been occurring in western Canada that great upsurge of political activity associated with the rise of the farmers' movement. Where Nova Scotia and Upper Canada, and the various other early rural communities in North America, had had their Religious Awakenings, in western Canada, or so it appeared, it was a Political Awakening which had aroused the population to action. A great new faith was born; people were given something to believe in and fight for. And if the successes achieved by the new political and co-operative movements on a community-wide basis stirred hopes of the coming of a better world in which to live, organization at the local level offered new rich experiences of community association which attracted the support of the whole population, old and young, male and female. The farmers' movements did go a long way during the 1920's to provide the people of western Canada with something to take the place of the church, and an observer in 1930 might well have concluded that there had occurred a general shift of the population to an acceptance of secular values.

There were a number of developments, however, which should

[2]C. A. Dawson, *Group Settlement: Ethnic Communities in Western Canada* (Toronto, 1936).

have provided a warning that such was not the case. If the churches in the western Canadian rural community had suffered a serious decline in strength, there were already indications by 1930 that the set back was temporary; with increasing maturity, new social supports of traditional religious organization were developing and over the next twenty-five years, and particularly the last ten of those years, much of the ground which had been lost by the churches in rural western Canada was being won back. On the other hand, the growth of the farmers' political movements did not involve as great a shift to secular values as has so often been supposed. The rise of the People's Church in close relationship to the western farmer and labour movements, the prominent part played in farmer and labour movements by men who in early life had been clergymen, and the strong ethical appeal of the farm and labour programmes of reform emphasized the extent to which the protest of the western Canadian population was directed against the kind of leadership being provided by the churches rather than against their basic teachings or principles.

Even more, the rapid growth of new religious movements in rural western Canada in the latter years of the 1920's, and the marked falling off in the strength of the farmers' political movements during these same years, indicated fairly clearly that what had been true of western Canada of the early 1920's was not likely to remain true. The first generation of western Canadians was passing, and with its passing profound changes were beginning to take place in the western Canadian rural community.

But these were developments, in 1930, no bigger than a man's hand. It was only after the depression began to make its effects felt that there could no longer be any mistaking what was taking place. The depression brought with it a terrible disillusionment. Loss of faith in the grand economic and political solutions which in the early 1920's had aroused such enthusiasm led to a violent reaction and a desperate search for new remedies for the ills of mankind. In Alberta, where hopes had developed the strongest, the reaction went the furthest, and here, during the very years Dawson and Younge were writing up their field notes for *Pioneering in the Prairie Provinces*, there occurred a great upsurge of religious feeling which, without much exaggeration, might be described as a Religious Awakening.

No one exploited more successfully than Mr. William Aberhart those social conditions in Alberta which favoured an appeal to religious values. Social Credit was not, of course, a purely religious movement, but its phenomenal growth during the early years of the 1930's certainly cannot be understood except in terms of the general strengthening of religious forces in the Alberta community. It was to Aberhart, the man of God, that people turned in these times of trouble rather than to Aberhart, the expounder of a new economic doctrine. The intimate mixing of politics and religion in his radio broadcasts and public speeches gave to his appeal its special force, and the election campaign of 1935 took on the character of a great religious crusade.

Social Credit quite clearly was a depression phenomenon. It would be hard to conceive that Aberhart, if still alive, could have made in the prosperous years of the 1940's or 1950's the kind of appeal he made in 1935; to keep in existence, the party he founded has had to change very much its basic character. But if Social Credit has ceased to be a party of economic protest, and if it has lost much of its crusading spirit, it would be a mistake to conclude from this that its growth in the 1930's represented only a temporary and short-lived break in the orderly political and religious development of Canada. Wild new political and religious movements, in most cases, can be counted upon to develop into respectable political parties and churches, but the emergence of still newer if not wilder movements can likewise be counted upon. Social Credit was not the first, and it is not likely to represent the last, challenge to the *status quo* in the political and religious organization of Canada.

S. D. CLARK

Preface

THE RESEARCH for this volume was carried out during the summers of 1946 and 1947, when the writer was working toward a Ph.D. in Sociology. Financial assistance was received through a grant from the Canadian Social Science Research Council. Delay in preparing the material for publication resulted from the author's absorption in theological studies and later in parish work as a priest of the Anglican Church.

Special thanks are due to Professor S. D. Clark, whose help and guidance from start to finish have been of inestimable value, and to Dr. Jean Burnet, also of the University of Toronto, for her work of editorial revision. Mrs. Rolland Estall, who aided in the research, was a constant inspiration and encouragement. I owe a great debt of thanks to my wife, whose determination, moral support, and editorial criticisms made possible the actual completion of the book. The editorial staff of the University of Toronto Press also rendered valuable service of an editorial nature. Dr. Morland P. Lamb, to whom the study is dedicated, supplied indispensable assistance at the end, by allowing me time to complete the writing while serving as his assistant at St. Cuthbert's Church, Leaside, Toronto.

WILLIAM E. MANN

Contents

SECT, CULT, AND CHURCH IN ALBERTA

CHAPTER ONE

Introduction

THE IMPACT OF SECT upon church in Canada for the period 1760 to 1900 has been examined in *Church and Sect in Canada*, by S. D. Clark.[1] This volume is intended to carry forward the sociological understanding of Canadian religious institutions by concentrating upon the ways in which both sects and cults emerged and expanded in Alberta at the expense of the more established churches. While this is the focus of attention, it was inevitable that considerable space be devoted to examination of the failures and shortcomings of the churches and how these contributed to the success of new religious movements. Although the period under scrutiny extends from 1887 to 1947, concentrated attention was paid to the years 1930 to 1947, as the period of greatest significance.

The principal reason for selecting Alberta for this study was its exceptional history of religious non-conformity, a history without contemporary parallel among the provinces of Canada. Though its sister provinces, Saskatchewan on the east and British Columbia on the west, had indeed given birth to a great variety of unorthodox religious movements, neither of them had produced such a bewildering mixture of competing religious organizations as Alberta. In this province were to be found not only all the customary evangelical bodies together with numerous older sects from Europe, such as the Mennonites, Hutterites, and Doukhobors, but also many other lesser-known sects and cults. Included in these were esoteric cults imported from California or the Canadian West Coast as well as a number of fundamentalist sects which actually got their start in Alberta. Altogether, in 1946, the province boasted of almost fifty different religious bodies exclusive of the traditional churches.

Alberta attracted attention not only by the variety of its religious groupings but also by the influential role which sectarian religion had played in political and social developments. In what other province of Canada had two successive premiers been active preachers and leaders in a fundamentalist evangelical movement? In what

[1]Toronto, 1948.

other province had the party in power maintained close, informal ties for, in 1947, twelve consecutive years with a small, little-known evangelical sect? The intimate and unbroken association of Alberta's Social Credit party and its leaders with the fundamentalist Prophetic Baptist Institute spoke clearly of extraordinary sectarian developments. Other religious trends had been almost as amazing. For instance, the non-denominational fundamentalist Bible school at Three Hills, Alberta, the Prairie Bible Institute, had in 1947 the largest daytime enrolment of any seminary or Bible school on the American continent. Since the early forties, it had been annually catechizing over a thousand students in old-fashioned puritanism and evangelicalism, and despatching them to spread these doctrines not only into every corner of the Prairies but also into lands across the sea. By 1950, the school boasted some 300 foreign missionaries. The extraordinary number of theological graduates turned out annually by the Prairie Bible Institute, combined with the output of the province's ten other sectarian seminaries, made Alberta the leading province in Canada for Bible school trained preachers. In the field of religious broadcasting, the province's sects and cults, together with certain independent "evangelical" ministers, had secured control of air time in a way unparalled in any other province. As early as the mid-thirties, two evangelical sects had achieved almost complete control of two of the province's six radio stations. By 1946, in addition to numerous Sunday programmes, two independent evangelists beamed daily half-hour revivalist programmes into every corner of Alberta, winning thousands of listeners. Again, sectarian strength in proportion to the population was quite exceptional. According to careful calculation, about 20 per cent of the Protestant population of Alberta in 1946 belonged to unorthodox religious movements; inasmuch as the percentage of "dead wood" on the rolls of the orthodox Protestant churches is admittedly higher than in the case of irregular religious bodies, the comparative strength of the latter was probably even greater than indicated by this percentage.

Within the general period under study, Alberta underwent a vast number of economic and social changes. Immigration, coming in waves before and after the First World War, brought the population up from 374,295 in 1911 to close to 900,000 by 1947. Rushes of settlement in farming areas switched the emphasis from cattle raising to grain production and after 1920 even the inhospitable Peace River district was opened to agricultural settlement. Early discoveries of oil and natural gas in the south were followed by the uncovering of important soft and hard coal deposits. Alberta's almost limitless resources and alternations of high prosperity and economic depression, especially in the period 1928–35, provided a continuous stimulus to changing patterns of settlement and socio-economic organization.

The general theoretical framework for this study is derived from hypotheses advanced in sociological literature on the sect and the cult. The sect is defined as a social institution distinguished from the church type of structure by certain basic social characteristics. These include an ascetic morality which renounces many so-called "worldly" values and mores, a vigorous protest against formality and conventionality in religious procedures, an attempt to recover the original and unadulterated essence of religion (in Christianity, to recover "pure" New Testament teachings), a high degree of equality and fraternity among the members along with an unusual degree of lay participation in worship and organizational activities. Sects are also usually exclusive and selective in membership and hence tend to be small and homogeneous. Sociological literature mentions other characteristics which, if not invariably found among these groups, are common to many. For example, sectarian groups tend to show great respect for leaders with charismatic powers and a casual indifference to, or an energetic protest against, the professionalization and hierarchization of the clergy. They are often suspicious of sacramental forms of theology and worship, such as infant baptism. This standpoint is usually accompanied by an emphasis upon individual religious experience, a requirement that generally limits full membership to adults. Furthermore, most sects rigidly eschew membership in the district councils of churches and the national associations of the Protestant denominations.

Sociologically, sects are generally viewed as institutions of social and religious protest,[2] as bulwarks of certain disadvantaged social groups in their struggle against the social power, moral conventions, and ethos of the middle classes, and against institutionalized and formalized religion. On the other hand, the church is considered to be a religious structure which has become well accommodated to the secular world, and is, for the most part, aligned with the middle and upper classes. Membership in the church is taken as a token of respectability. Thus, while the spirit of the church is largely this-worldly and accommodative, that of the sect is distrustful of the secular world and its supporters, and is basically separatist.

Times of rapid social change usually produce new sects. In such

[2]J. Wach, *Sociology of Religion* (Chicago, 1940), p. 104.

periods, settled relationships between classes and institutions are greatly disturbed, social integration is threatened, and ultimately a portion of the population finds itself on the fringe of the organized social structure. The general social unrest provokes new social needs, especially among groups most exposed to acute dislocation.[3] The established churches, owing to the "sheltered" existence of the majority of members and clergy, commonly fail to adjust adequately to the situation. Thus it is that sects may emerge, having as their social purpose the defence of the interests and needs of marginal sections of the population.

While sociologists have written voluminously on the sect, as yet they have devoted little attention to cult groups, such as Unity Truth, the I Am, and Rosicrucianism. In spite of its comprehensiveness Wach's *The Sociology of Religion* overlooks most of these new groups, while discussing a few of them, under the rather vague term "independent group."[4] A more helpful introduction to these institutions is found in a couple of paragraphs in Wiese and Becker's *Systematic Sociology*. Here it is pointed out: "Tendencies toward religion of a strictly private, personal character . . . come to full fruition in the cult . . . an amorphous, loose-textured, uncondensed type of social structure."[5] Professor W. W. Sweet advances an analytical distinction between cults and sects which is helpful if somewhat limited in its usefulness:

A cult is a religious group which looks for its basic and peculiar authority outside the Christian tradition. Generally, cults accept Christianity, but often only as a halfway station on the road to a greater "truth" and profess to have a new and additional authority beyond Christianity. This new authority may be a relevation which constitutes additional "scriptures" or it may be an inspired leader who announces that he or she has gained additional insight into "truth."[6]

Thus, whereas sects emphasize recovery of primitive, first-century Christian doctrine, cults tend to blend alien religious or psychological notions with Christian doctrine with a view to obtaining a more "adequate" or "modern" faith. For this reason they are labelled

[3]L. Pope, *Millhands and Preachers* (New Haven, 1942).
[4]Wach, *Sociology of Religion*, pp. 194–6.
This is the term used by Joachim Wach to describe certain religious bodies that lie outside the sect or church category. "The adoption of its own principle of organization is the distinctive feature marking the development of an independent group."
[5]Leopold von Wiese and H. Becker, *Systematic Sociology* (New York, 1932), p. 627.
[6]W. W. Sweet, *American Culture and Religion* (Dallas, 1951), p. 93. See also W. E. Garrison, *The March of Faith* (New York, 1933), pp. 275–6.

heresies by both the churches and the sects and especially denounced by the latter. It is this blending or syncretic feature which distinguishes the cults, including Christian Science, Unity Truth, and Theosophy, from established churches and from recognized sects, and at the same time constitutes the principal basis of their religious separation. As each Christian sect "justifies" its existence by concentrating upon one or more neglected elements of Christian teaching, so each cult attempts to "defend" its right to independent existence by selecting slightly different elements of the Christian religion to *combine* with non-Christian notions.

Besides this syncretism, cults are found to possess a number of other common characteristics. Their services are generally lacking in stirring emotional manifestations; dramatic exhortations or preaching are consistently eschewed and new members are won by "reasoned" or speculative argument rather than by emotional appeals. Most cults accept the validity of modern science and its assumption of a rational cosmic system. In a sense, these groups are post-scientific in outlook, and professedly metaphysical, while sects and churches are pre-scientific. On the other hand, as "meta-physical" bodies, the cults represent a protest against purely physical science and all forms of crass materialism. Their role is to emphasize the value of speculative and mentalistic (mind over body) knowledge. Opposed to elaborate ceremony, in form of organization they tend to be rational and business-like. Again, whereas the sect is indifferent or opposed to many secular goals such as worldly prestige, popularity, and wealth, the cults often tacitly accept and come to terms with just such values. In this sense, they are adjusted to the secular culture and are therefore utilitarian and this-worldly in outlook. Their attitude to the established churches is generally one of condescension or enlightened superiority. They consider that they have discovered new truth which the churches will eventually be forced to accept.

Cults are further distinguished from sectarian bodies by their moral outlook. Seldom do they take a strong ascetic stand or press upon their followers a programme of strict moral self-denial. "Instead of righteousness, the [cult's] goal of action is harmony, happiness and success."[7] In membership regulations they are less rigid and exclusive than sects. The same is true of their attitude toward the Holy Scriptures. In fact, the conventional cult approach to Holy Writ, far from being literalistic and rigid, is quite speculative and allegorical. Cult

[7]G. G. Atkins, *Modern Cults and Religious Movements* (New York, 1923), p. 240.

leaders also differ markedly from leaders of other religious bodies; while often lacking the organizational acumen of church ministers and the emotional fluidity of sectarian preachers, they tend to possess a type of charisma compounded of personal charm and speculative or imaginative gifts. It is significant too that women predominate among cult leaders. All these common features suggest that modern cults constitute a distinctive socio-religious group, blending something of the accommodative spirit of the church with eclectic and individualistic features to make a new kind of religious structure.

In carrying out this study, a strenuous effort was made to penetrate into the essential facts about the historical development of each sect and cult and most of the non-Roman churches[8] in Alberta. Closest attention was paid to first-hand source materials. A mass of data pertaining to the social and economic developments in the province and their apparent relationship to changes in religious organization was sought out. It was assumed that new religious bodies would only make headway if they met significant social needs and this assumption directed much of the enquiry. The enquiry proceeded with an attitude of sympathy for the viewpoint and driving motivation of each of the new groups, along with an effort to appreciate the peculiarities of the Alberta social scene. It was clear that only by viewing the religious developments in Alberta against the background of frontier expansion and community instability could anyone begin to understand the social roots of resurgent sect and cult movements.

[8]The development of the Roman Catholic Church was not examined owing to its remoteness from Protestant sectarianism as well as practical difficulties of observation.

CHAPTER TWO

The History of Sects and Cults in Alberta

SECTS AND CULTS made an appearance in what was to become the province of Alberta at the very beginning of settlement.[1] As the population grew, they increased also, both in number and in membership,[2] and by the 1940's had become a significant part of the religious organization of the province.

Four sects had established themselves in the area by 1900: the Salvation Army, the German Baptist Church of North America, the Mennonites, and the Evangelical Swedish Mission Covenant of America. The Salvation Army was the first sect to arrive, getting its start among pioneers from eastern Canada. It began work in Calgary in 1887, and "twenty-four soldiers were enrolled in the first three months."[3] In 1909 it erected a hall with a seating capacity of 700. Centres were also opened in several other towns. By 1911, according to the census, the Army had 1,082 supporters in Alberta. After rising to 1,773 by 1921, membership increased by only 251 in the next decade and 71 between 1931 and 1941.[4]

In 1892 the fundamentalist German Baptist Church of North America started a congregation at a village called Rabbit Hill. Until 1914, it grew rapidly in the Edmonton area among German-speaking Russians and German Americans. In 1920, it had 1,350 adult members in 17 congregations, and in 1937, chiefly because of immigration sponsored after 1926 by the sect's American branch, 2,194 members

[1]The history and theological roots of nearly all the groups dealt with in this study are described in the latest edition of E. T. Clark, *The Small Sect in America* (Nashville, Tenn., 1937).

[2]Membership figures given are often only approximate. Census figures concerning religious affiliation are not precise or detailed. The religious groups themselves, especially in their early years, often did not keep records; if they did, they rarely counted regular adherents as well as members. As most research was done in the Calgary area, figures for Calgary were secured wherever provincial statistics were unobtainable.

[3]From a history written by the local unit of the Calgary Salvation Army.

[4]Membership figures for this and other religious bodies for 1911, 1921, 1931, and 1941 are from Dominion Bureau of Statistics, *Eighth Census of Canada, 1941*, and preceding censuses, unless otherwise specified.

and 20 churches. In 1939 the group opened in Edmonton the Christian Training Institute, designed to teach Baptist doctrine and to encourage young men to enter the ministry. Subsequent growth, however, was not spectacular: between 1937 and 1945, the sect won only 233 members.

The first Mennonites to enter Alberta arrived in 1892 from Manitoba, settling north of Calgary at Carstairs and Didsbury. In the next few years they were joined by small parties of fellow-believers from Ontario and Russia. Later, still more arrived, so that the total strength of the sect jumped from 522 in 1901 to 1,535 in 1911; and in 1923 a group of Russian-born Mennonites settled near Lethbridge. There were about 6,000 Mennonites in Alberta in 1931, and 8,000 in 1941.[5] By 1941 they were divided into six factions, the Old Colony, the Mennonite Brethren in Christ, the Old Order Mennonites, the Church of God in Christ (Haldermanites), the General Conference Mennonites, and the Evangelical Mennonite Brethren. The last two were numerically the strongest.

In 1894 the little-known group called the Swedish Evangelical Mission Covenant of America[6] began services in the village of New Sweden, south of Edmonton. Expansion was insignificant, although some advance was made between 1925 and 1935. In 1935 membership in the three prairie provinces reached 603. A period of growth beginning in the late thirties was cut short in 1945 by a doctrinal controversy which originated in the sect's prairie Bible school.[7] By 1946, there were approximately 300 adult members of the Swedish Evangelical Mission Covenant in Alberta.

The flood of migration into Alberta after the turn of the century led directly to the appearance of six more unusual religious movements. In 1902, a small group of German-American settlers began meetings of the Church of the Brethren or Dunkards in the villages of Pleasant Valley and Seven Persons near Medicine Hat. In the next ten years, planned emigration from the United States brought over several new congregations. A western Canadian "district" was organized in

[5]Round figures are unavoidable since the census lumps Mennonites and Hutterites together.

[6]First emerged in North America on July 4, 1868, at Swede Bend, Iowa; the denomination was officially founded in Chicago in 1885. For further historical treatment see George M. Stephenson, *Religious Aspects of Swedish Immigration* (University of Minnesota Press).

[7]See superintendent's report in *Swedish Evangelical Mission Covenant Yearbook*, 1946, p. 8: "I believe we already this year have lost many opportunities of winning souls to Christ because our mind has been more set on defending a particular view of the Atonement than for reaching out for lost souls around us. This has almost certainly meant the loss of God's blessing upon our work in Canada."

1919, with half of its membership of 500 residing in Alberta. During 1921 and 1922, special evangelistic services added about a hundred followers, but after 1933 interest waned until, in 1945, there were only 300 Dunkards in the prairies, and in Alberta, only two of the original five congregations continued to meet. Rev. E. C. Cawley, Alberta secretary for the sect, in a letter to the author, attributed this decline to missionary policies pursued by the theologically liberal "Mother" congregations in the United States which failed to furnish ministers and literature suitable to the religious communities of Alberta. Mr. Cawley wrote:

Since about 1933, the church in Canada has depended upon pastors from the States, a free (i.e. unpaid) ministry being no longer available or adequate. These have been the years of greatest difficulty. The second and third generations have had but little contact with the main body of the church, and the church literature does not meet our needs here. In 1934, a pastor from the States, Rev. John Wieand, a far-sighted leader who profited by the experience of other and larger denominations in Canada, began a Biblical and Leaders' school for the training of *native* leaders. This was eagerly supported by the young embryonic leaders but lack of support from many of the older members, as well as outright opposition, forced the closing of the school. Wieand returned to the States and in two years most of the more promising young leaders had followed him.

Our experience with the American Pastors has not been too successful. Only a few have remained as much as three years; therefore, they are gone before becoming "acclimated" to our different political customs and the somewhat different trends and religious conceptions in general. They are somewhat inclined to consider Canada an adjunct to the U.S., which idea just will not go hand in hand with success for their pastoral work. So the years since 1935 have been the ones of greatest difficulty. [The mission board leaders] see only the likeness between the U.S. and Canada and not the few but vital differences and their underlying significance. [August 23, 1947.]

Calgary followers of the Raven-ite "exclusive" faction of the schismatic Plymouth Brethren sect first organized meetings in 1903. The next year a congregation of the "Open" Brethren, so called largely because they were less strict concerning membership qualifications, also started meeting in Calgary. The charter members for both these groups came principally from Ontario. In the next few years, the "Open" congregation grew steadily but the Raven faction declined as some of its members left for the Coast. In 1910, a third Brethren group, the Gladdon-ites, began services in Calgary. Census figures indicate that the three factions together had 279 supporters in Alberta in 1914, 426 in 1921, 528 in 1931, and 464 in 1941. However, in 1941, although the census listed only 94 Brethren in Calgary, the groups themselves reported a combined membership of 225, the Open Brethren having 170 members, the Gladdon party 10, and the Raven-ites 50. The reluctance of many Brethren to accept precise sectarian

labelling may have led some to describe themselves to census takers
as Gospel people rather than Plymouth Brethren. Whatever the
correct membership figure, it was probably little different from that
of 1921.

In 1905, the Church of Christ, which split off from the American
Disciples of Christ in 1874 and since then has itself split at least four
ways, sprang up in Calgary. The congregation began with eight
members and grew very slowly, losing some supporters to the Disciples
of Christ in 1913. It had 25 followers by 1920 and then simply held
on. In 1946, the sect, still limited to the lone Calgary congregation,
had fewer than 30 adult members in Alberta.

A Church of Christ Scientist was begun in 1906 at Edmonton, and
another in Calgary the next year. The first members were largely
Anglo-Saxons from eastern Canada and the United States. By 1911,
the movement had 515 followers in Alberta. In the next decade a
wave of Christian Science swept the prairies and membership trebled
in each western province, reaching 2,154 in Alberta. The census then
records 1,728 followers in 1931 and 1,733 in 1941. Christian Science
officials will release no membership statistics for recent years, and
deny that a decline has occurred, but the fact that one of their two
Calgary congregations collapsed during the twenties lends support
to the census report.[8]

A Seventh Day Adventist congregation emerged at Calgary in
1906 among a small settlement of Russian Germans from the Dakotas.
As more German-speaking settlers entered Alberta, other congregations were quickly formed. Work was begun in 1909 on a residential
college at Lacombe, subsequently named the Canadian Junior College.[9] Owing to intensified evangelistic activities, the number of
members increased to 3,533 by 1921. By this time the sect was attracting settlers of Ukrainian, Scandinavian and British origin. Since then,
in spite of the growing influence of their college, which by 1946
had an enrolment of around 350, the Adventists have registered little

[8]The Committee on Publications of Alberta will release no membership figures,
and yet it maintained that the census records do not give a faithful account of
its Alberta development. In a letter to the author dated August 7, 1947, H. T.
Logan, Secretary of the Committee on Publications of Alberta, wrote: "In spite of
the Canadian census or any other material estimates, I can truly say to you that
Christian Science is not declining in the West. There are other ways aside from
figures of forming opinions and reaching sound convictions on such questions. . . .
After all, churches and religions must be judged less from the material standpoint
and more from the spiritual." Other prairie provinces seem not to follow the Alberta
trend, but to show a slight increase in Christian Scientists. The census figures for
all of Canada indicate a small gain between 1931 and 1941.
[9]Their other college is at Oshawa, Ontario.

advance. Their numbers increased by only 680 from 1921 to 1931, by 484 in the next ten years, and by 87 between 1941 and 1946. The migration of some members to British Columbia and the loss of others owing to a stand of uncompromising pacifism, helps to explain this levelling off of membership.

Another sect which started among German-speaking settlers was the Evangelical United Brethren, a group with a Methodist, pietistic standpoint. Missionaries from eastern Canada began labours on the prairies in 1907 and by 1911 the sect had 1,032 followers in Alberta. The number had grown to 1,626 by 1921, partly through conversions from Lutheranism. Expansion was limited in the twenties but picked up in the thirties after a Bible college was opened at Regina. The census credits the Evangelical United Brethren with 2,133 followers in 1931 and 4,165 in 1941. There was steady growth during the war years and by 1946 the sect was one of the largest fundamentalist groups in the province.

The wave of migration that swept into Alberta in the years immediately preceding 1914 contributed to the appearance of thirteen new religious groups. Three "holiness" groups with almost identical doctrines, the Free Methodists, the Holiness Movement, and the Nazarenes, appeared in the years 1910 and 1911. Starting in Calgary in 1910, with a mere handful of supporters, the Free Methodists had organized eight churches in the province by 1925. Most of these were located in small towns west of Edmonton. After 1930 growth was negligible and in 1946 the sect claimed only 221 adult members and eleven congregations. This limited expansion may be related to the retention of certain so-called original Methodist customs, such as kneeling on the floor for prayer and the tabooing of instrumental music. The following paragraph from a field report on a Free Methodist service shows a visitor's reaction to these old-fashioned procedures:

Everyone knelt on the floor for the prayer, resting their elbows on the seats of their chairs. The prayer seemed endless because of the extreme hardness of the floor and I was on the verge of screaming with pain by the time we were finally allowed to rise. . . . The entire service was uninspiring and dull. An atmosphere of gloom and tediousness prevailed. The people were apathetic and listless. . . . As for myself, I was completely bored.

The Holiness Movement, which had split off from the Methodist Church in 1886 under the Rev. Ralph Horner,[10] entered Alberta in 1911, and organized a few congregations during the First World

[10]The Rev. Ralph Horner led this group out of the Methodist Church in Ontario. See S. D. Clark, Church and Sect in Canada (Toronto, 1948), pp. 368-78.

War, mainly in the north. A schism, which led to the formation of the Standard Church of America in 1918, resulted in the loss of several congregations. The census credited the Holiness Movement with only 160 followers in 1921. There was an increase to 252 by 1931, but only four followers were added in the next decade, and in 1947 the total adult membership did not exceed 150. The Standard Church on the other hand, claimed, by 1931, thirteen preaching places and a hundred adult members in Alberta.[11] In 1946, it had half a dozen congregations and 300 adherents and members, including children. It, like the Holiness Movement, was strongest in northern Alberta.

In 1911, also, a congregation of the Church of the Nazarene was started in Calgary with fourteen members. Originating in the northwestern United States, in the beginning this group attracted chiefly Anglo-Saxon settlers from eastern Canada. Growth was slow at first but by 1926 there were 499 adult members in 17 congregations. Two years later a Bible school was erected at Red Deer. During the early depression years expansion was more rapid: in 1933 alone, 136 new members were added. From 1938 to 1942 membership increased by 389, new congregations being organized at the rate of one a year. In 1945 the sect boasted 1,395 adult members in 43 preaching places. Indeed, by this year, owing to a daily radio broadcast from Calgary, the addition of a High School department to the Red Deer Bible College, and the able leadership of the district superintendent, the Rev. E. Lawlor, this sect had become one of the leading evangelical forces in Alberta.

Another American-born group, the Disciples of Christ, began services in Calgary in 1913. In the United States and most provinces of Canada this body, organized in Canada under the name of the All-Canada Disciples of Christ, had lost its sectarian characteristics by the thirties, but in Alberta a fundamentalist and evangelical emphasis was still uppermost in 1946. The pioneer Calgary congregation secured over 100 members within a year. By 1916 there were 11 preaching points in the province and 586 adult members. Membership thereafter fluctuated widely: it fell to 407 in 1917, increased to 624 in 1920, and fell again to 432 in 1926. During these years there was a serious shortage of clergy. Subsequently membership picked up and then increased rapidly during the early thirties, reaching 800 in 1933. In that year, the Rev. C. H. Phillips established a Bible college in Lethbridge and in 1942 led the majority of the pastors

---

[11]F. E. Howley-James, "A History of the Development of the Church and Religious Education in Alberta," B. D. thesis, University of Alberta, 1935.

and congregations in Alberta out of the All-Canada Disciples in protest against tendencies toward modernism and centralization. Since 1942 Phillips' Bible school has supplied the Alberta congregations with a flow of new pastors. However, the group failed to exhibit steady expansion, membership in 1946 remaining still around 800.[12]

Some time between 1910 and 1914 the curious and little-known Cooneyites,[13] popularly called the "Two by Two's" on the prairies, were started in Alberta. This sect attempts to propagate exclusively the Christianity of the Book of Acts, using the evangelistic methods set forward in this book. They have no paid clergy and pursue all missionary work by itinerant lay evangelists, about half of them women, who carry no purse or script but seek hospitality from fellow-believers and are financed by friendly gifts. Owing to their profound distaste for publicity, their growth is hard to trace. They seem to have expanded gradually at first, and then to have made relatively faster headway during the depression. By 1946 they had about a hundred followers in Calgary and between 1,200 and 1,800 in the province.

Around 1910 four millenial sects organized congregations in Calgary. One of these was the Christadelphians or Brethren of Christ, a group which emphasizes the second coming of Christ and the prophetic use of the Scriptures, and rejects the idea of hell. Its early supporters were recent immigrants from eastern Canada or England. The Calgary congregation grew very slowly; and in 1921 there were only 88 Christadelphians, including children, in the province. The emergence of tiny congregations in Edmonton, Claresholm, and Lethbridge brought this figure up to 136 by 1931. Since then the sect has expanded neither in Alberta nor generally in Canada. One field worker observed:

I seriously doubt if they [Christadelphians] desire universal Christadelphianism. The members are fond of saying that everyone is not capable of "seeing the light." Therefore they are not given to any enthusiastic evangelistic schemes. [Moreover] their appeal is neither emotional nor aesthetic. Their services are extremely prosaic. . . . They attempt to appeal to reason rather than to emotion. They emphasize good living and intense Bible study—and regard the Bible as a sort of mysterious puzzle book, from which, by means of great study and ingenuity, the answers to all problems can be discovered.

During the First World War, the early meetings of British Israel, whose millenial outlook associates the second coming of Christ with the triumph of the British Empire, occasionally attracted over a

[12]The census figures for this sect, which retained the name Disciples of Christ, are particularly unreliable, since they include many scattered individuals some of whom still owe allegiance to the All-Canada denomination.

[13]For additional information see page 26.

hundred persons in Calgary; one meeting in 1919 is said to have drawn more than 300. Interest waned during the twenties, but revived after 1930 when the Rev. E. J. Springett was made Dominion Commissioner. Depression conditions, coupled with Springett's leadership, meant, in the words of one leading member, that "people just flocked to the meetings" in both Calgary and Edmonton. The movement took on a more institutional form, kept membership lists, charged annual dues and even opened a book-store in Calgary. During the Second World War some Calgary rallies were attended by several hundred people. For lack of full-time leadership, however, the group failed to build up membership in the smaller centres. In 1946 its small Alberta following was concentrated in Calgary and Edmonton.

The Reorganized Church of the Latter Day Saints of Jesus Christ, a Mormon group which rejected such teachings of the Utah branch as polygamy, celestial marriage, Adam-God worship, baptisms for the dead, and the secret Temple rites, first began in Calgary in 1910 among people who had come from Ontario.[14] The sect grew very slowly, adding small units at Ribstone and Edmonton in the twenties. By 1930 its Alberta membership, including children of eight years and over, had reached 593. Since then, there has been no significant expansion.[15]

A fourth millenial group, the Russellites or International Bible Students, later called Jehovah's Witnesses, began meetings in Calgary around 1910. The main beliefs that Russell tirelessly reiterated were that the imminent second coming of Christ would bring rewards to the faithful and that the idea of a fiery hell was without scriptural basis. Beginning with 86 supporters in 1911, the Russellite movement increased to 627 by 1921, in spite of the death of Pastor Russell in 1916 and a period of internal schism. Under Judge Rutherford's leadership it grew rapidly and by 1931 the census recorded 1,252 "Bible Students," some of whom were apparently independent Russellites unattached to the main organization. Ten years later, when the Jehovah's Witnesses had been declared illegal because of their stand against war, the census reported 1,010, but it is doubtful if this figure represented even 50 per cent of their real strength. In 1947

[14]A brief but lucid account of the early history of this sect and of the differences between it and the Utah Mormons is given in the pamphlets, *Latter Day Glory* and *Differences that Matter* by E. A. Smith.

[15]The sect follows the same practice as the Utah group of sending out lay missionaries in two's, but has not had in recent years as many people willing to do this work.

headquarters claimed about 1,000 publishers in the province, about half of whom were concentrated in Calgary and Edmonton. Since publishers were required to undertake twelve hours of "publishing" work per week, and included therefore only the most zealous of the adult supporters of the movement, the total number of followers in 1947, including children, was probably in the neighbourhood of 3,000.

Four cults also took root in Alberta just before the First World War. The Spiritualists began meeting in Calgary around 1911, when a medium named Mrs. Duval arrived there. During the war at least four mediums operated in the city and at their peak probably had a combined following of 350 to 450 persons.[16] Interest waned soon after the end of hostilities and the 1921 census reported only 210 followers. In the twenties three groups combined into one and two new societies were organized. In spite of this activity, the census reported only 197 Spiritualists in 1931. There was a short-lived revival of interest in Spiritualism during the depression and the early part of the Second World War. By 1946, however, there were only about 80 people in the two active groups of Spiritualists in Calgary,[17] and a few in Edmonton.

In 1911 Rosicrucianism[18] came to Calgary in the form of a branch of the Rosicrucian Fellowship, one of the three main Rosicrucian groups. During the twenties it grew to about 30 members. In the early thirties dissension at headquarters in California, a split in the local group, and the appeal of a new cult, the I Am, led to a decline. A slight recovery occurred during the war years so that by 1946 there were again about 30 members, chiefly middle-aged women of Anglo-Saxon heritage. The schismatic lodge of the thirties was probably a branch of the American Order of the Rosy Cross (AMORC). Up to 1946 it had only a very small following. Rosicrucianism in Alberta was virtually confined to Calgary.

The first lodge of Theosophists[19] was opened in Calgary in 1913, starting with seven persons who had formerly belonged to the city's "Metaphysical Library," rising to 50 by 1914, and falling to 30 in 1920. A split in 1923 led to the formation of a rival group called the Krishna lodge, which specialized in the study of comparative religion, while the first group concentrated upon astrological insights. By 1946 the original lodge had about 10 followers, the Krishna lodge twenty,

[16]They led the following groups: the Western Star, the Independent Psychic Research Society, the Temple of Spiritual Light, and the First Spiritualist Church.
[17]These were the Independent Spiritualists and the First Spiritualist Church.
[18]Cf. C. W. Ferguson, *The Confusion of Tongues* (New York, 1928), p. 458.
[19]Cf. C. S. Braden, *These Also Believe* (New York, 1949).

and the Trinity lodge, organized after a schism in the Krishna lodge in 1932, another twenty. There was also a lodge of about twenty members in Edmonton.

About 1910, Swedenborg's Church of the New Jerusalem[20] came to Alberta. Swedenborg repudiated many basic Christian doctrines and rejected moral asceticism; his beliefs in the nature of evil and the after life were more oriental than Christian. This cult had 50 followers in 1911, mostly Swedish-American in background. They failed to expand and in 1946 claimed but one congregation in the province at a village called Sunny Slope.

The period 1914-21 saw a fresh upthrust of sectarian religion. Loosely centralized Pentecostal groups sprang up in rural areas, while non-denominational fundamentalist congregations emerged in the big cities. Representative of the latter were the People's Church[21] and The Church in Calgary.

The first distinctive sects to begin in this period were the Hutterites and Doukhobors. The census reports 45 Doukhobors in 1911, but the first bloc settlement of these extraordinary people in Alberta did not occur until 1916. In that year two groups totalling approximately 300 left their British Columbia colony at Brilliant and settled in western Alberta at Cowley and Lundbeck.[22] In 1924, another congregation parted company from the British Columbia colony owing to a dispute over the successor to their deceased leader, Peter Verigin. It was led by an illiterate woman named Anastasia who took several hundred followers to Arrowwood, Alberta, and called her movement "The Lordly Christian Community of Universal Brotherhood." By 1931, the census reported 786 Doukhobors in Alberta. In the next decade, their numbers increased to 822. In contrast to their fellow-believers in British Columbia, these Alberta Spirit-Wrestlers have aroused little publicity, favourable or unfavourable.

Not so fortunate were the Hutterites,[23] who first entered Alberta in 1918. Ten colonies of these people came up from South Dakota and settled in the south, continuing that restless search for security and social isolation that had taken them since 1622 from Moravia in and out of six different countries. By 1947, Hutterite fertility and

---

[20]Cf. Irvine, *Heresies Exposed*, and Ferguson, *The Confusion of Tongues*.

[21]Dr. Oswald Smith of Toronto was apparently the originator of the People's Churches, which drew much support from Methodists of a working-class background.

[22] C. A. Dawson, *Group Settlement: Ethnic Communities in Western Canada* (Toronto, 1936), pp. 40, 80–1. The official name of the Doukhobors is "The Christian Community of Universal Brotherhood."

[23]Their full name is The Hutterian Brethren.

further migrations from South Dakota brought their strength up to 35 colonies[24] and 4,039 followers. Post-war efforts to buy more farm land to take care of this expansion provoked a storm of hostile criticism and in April, 1947, the Alberta legislature passed a bill restricting their right—and that of the Doukhobors—to acquire further land. The sect was subjected to sharp criticism on many sides, but certain bodies, including the Civil Liberties Association of Canada, sprang to their defence.[25] It was emphasized that Alberta's Hutterites held only 45 acres of land per person, an acreage considerably below the per capita average among prairie farmers. At this writing, the law has not been changed, and it appears as if the Hutterites will soon be obliged to migrate elsewhere.[26]

In 1917 the Evangelical Free Church, a little-known group originating in the mid-western States among the Scandinavians as an offshoot of the Lutheran Church, started a congregation at Enchant, a town near Lethbridge. Growth was very slow and when a prairie-wide association was formed in 1928, it had only 80 members. Interest picked up in the years 1929 to 1933 and 1937 to 1946, and by the mid-forties there were seven congregations and 200 members, concentrated mainly in towns east and northeast of Lethbridge.

The beginnings of the Pentecostal Assemblies of Canada in Alberta can be traced to spontaneous "Holy Ghost" rallies that originated in the province's larger cities in the year 1916, when similar outbursts of evangelical emotionalism were occurring in other parts of Canada, in the United States, and in Lutheran areas of Europe.[27] The formal organization of the Pentecostal Assemblies of Canada took place in 1919. Early growth in Alberta was slow because of competition with other pentecostal associations such as the Gospel Tabernacle and the Assemblies of God.[28] In the late twenties, however, the Pentecostal Assemblies of Canada forged ahead, absorbing some competing groups and drawing upon its Western Bible College in Winnipeg for trained pastors. By 1931 it probably had 1,200 adult members. In the early depression years it opened up German-speaking churches in the area south of Edmonton and also attracted numbers

[24]Colonies are kept to a standard size of 150, or approximately 20 families.
[25]See vol. I, no. 2 of the *Manitoba Bulletin* of The Civil Liberties Association, 1947–8.
[26]For an analysis of the Hutterite social structure, see L. E. Deets, "The Hutterites, a Study in Social Cohesion," unpublished Ph.D. thesis, Columbia University Library.
[27]Cf. S. H. Fordsham, *With Signs Following* (Springfield, Mo., 1941).
[28]This is the name of the largest pentecostal movement in the United States. Cf. B. J. Oliver, "Some Newer Religious Groups in the U.S.A." (Ph.D. thesis, Yale University, 1946).

of Scandinavians and Ukrainians. One of its pastors likened his sect in this period to a sponge, which "picks up whatever is lying around loose." Expansion in the ten years prior to 1946 was steady but generally unspectacular, although a summer camp on Sylvan Lake, opened in 1936, attracted as many as 1,500 persons in one week. Membership in 1946 was approximately 2,000 excluding children.[29]

During the 1920's several new sects established themselves in Alberta. The Christian and Missionary Alliance, commonly called "the Alliance," entered the province around 1922. Early congregations were principally in rural areas and drew in former Methodists and members of the United Church. In 1931 the census credited the Alliance with 168 followers. After 1935 it spurted forward, aided by clever use of the Edmonton airwaves. Numerous new congregations were started in northern Alberta. A Bible school at Regina, opened in 1941, provided a steady supply of young pastors who went into remote rural communities. In 1941 the census reported 625 adherents, and by 1946 the Alliance had about 30 congregations and 1,700 followers, including children, in the province.[30]

In 1922 the Canadian prairies produced its first important native-born sect, the Apostolic Church of Pentecost, which broke off from the Pentecostal Assemblies of Canada, under Pastor Small of Winnipeg. Beginning with a small congregation in Calgary, the sect made little progress in Alberta until the late thirties. Then it developed a strong congregation in Edmonton, and in 1946 opened a small Bible school. Meantime, about half a dozen rural congregations had taken shape, mostly in the Peace River area. A large proportion of its following in both rural and urban areas was of Ukrainian, German, and Scandinavian extraction. In the absence of any membership records, it is estimated that the total Apostolic following in 1946, including children, was about 700. There were about 100 members in Calgary, 300 in Edmonton, 150 in Brownvale, and 450 in 6 smaller congregations.

The Church of God, Anderson, Ind., an American "holiness" sect

[29]Neither census nor membership statistics give a clear picture of the strength of the Pentecostal Assemblies of Canada. The census, which gives a figure of 8,451 in 1941, lumps all pentecostal groups together, including supporters of the Apostolic Church of Pentecost and the Pentecostal Holiness sect. The membership figure, 1,400 in 1946, includes only actual signed-up members, excluding a large number of regular adherents who for one reason or another do not officially belong.

[30]Official figures were unobtainable from the District Superintendent because of his long illness during 1946 and 1947. The Calgary and Edmonton congregations together had some 650 supporters by 1946.

founded to unite all Protestants, entered Alberta around 1924.[31] It grew slowly at first, mainly in the area near Edmonton and Wetaskawin, with settlers of German-American extraction making up the bulk of its membership. In 1932, a Bible school was erected at Camrose. From then on the sect expanded more rapidly. By 1946 it had 15 congregations and approximately 500 members excluding children, about half of German extraction.

One of the tiny splinter pentecostal groups to emerge in Alberta was the Church of the First Century, which started at Calgary in 1925 as the Emmanuel Mission. In the beginning the group had a reputation for wild and exciting services and attracted a congregation of 60 to 80 people. In the early thirties the original leader of the group resigned. The new leader introduced more restraint into the meetings and changed its name but was unable to prevent a fall in membership. By 1945 the congregation had dwindled to about 20 persons and leaders of Calgary's other pentecostal groups were looking toward the day when it would cease meeting and they would receive its members.

Unity Truth, a cult akin to Christian Science, began meeting in Calgary in 1926. Between 1926 and 1930 scores of people showed some interest in Unity but the actual membership never exceeded 30. In 1930 a trained minister was imported from the United States, and Calgary's membership rose in five years to about 100. Meanwhile, a group in Edmonton had secured about 40 supporters. After 1935, both the Calgary and Edmonton congregations lost members to two new cults with similar teachings, the Church of Truth and I Am, and by 1946 the combined membership of the two units had fallen to about 60. Unity headquarters in Kansas City, Missouri, stated that Alberta subscribers to their literature grew from 1,500 in 1930 to 3,000 in 1949,[32] but it is doubtful if as many as 1,000 of the 3,000 subscribers could be reckoned as Unity supporters.

In the early twenties several short-lived cult groups started up in Calgary whose brief existence indicated something of the unsettled conditions of those years. Shortly after 1920, a Hermes lodge was started among some of the former members of the Calgary Metaphysical Society. By 1923 it had grown to about 25 members. In the 1930's its leader left town, the group disbanded, and its supporters

[31]It was often confused with another sect of similar name and doctrine, The Church of God, Cleveland, Tenn. According to E. T. Clark, there are "a dozen sects in this country [the United States] claiming the title 'Church of God.'" *The Small Sect in America*, p. 129.

[32]In a letter dated August 4, 1949.

attached themselves to such groups as the Rosicrucians and the Theosophists. In 1925, Baron Ferson, allegedly a relative of Tolstoy, visited Calgary and lectured at the Palliser Hotel on behalf of a Light Bearer's Movement. A local group was organized which had about a hundred members by 1929. With the resignation of its Calgary leader, who subsequently attached herself to a series of different cults, this group also collapsed. Other such movements emerged in the same period only to meet a similar fate.

In 1927, the Prophetic Baptist movement, which later gave birth to the Social Credit party, was founded by William Aberhart. Biblical prophecy and fundamentalist literalism were its two distinctive emphases. At the outset it was simply a Sunday afternoon Bible class which Aberhart had begun teaching in 1918, at the Westbourne Baptist Church in Calgary. As the numbers increased, the class left the Church and met in the larger theatres in town. By 1925, when he started to broadcast, Aberhart had several hundred regular followers, and soon his influence within the fundamentalist Westbourne congregation began to overshadow that of its minister. Two years later, with contributions from his radio audience, he built a $65,000 church capable of seating 1,200 people. At this point, he won over a large proportion of the Westbourne congregation, and virtually directed all important activities. In 1929 when a majority of the former Westbourne congregation withdrew in disillusionment over Aberhart's leadership, he named his group the Bible Institute Baptist Church and without ordination took over as pastor. To co-ordinate all the broadcasting operations he organized separately the Calgary Prophetic Bible Institute, which listed, in 1929, 700 urban and 1,085 rural supporters, and a radio Sunday School of 1,200.[33] At its peak in 1935, Aberhart's religious radio audience was computed at 300,000,[34] the Bible Institute listed 1,275 supporters, the Calgary church had over 500 adult members, the radio Sunday school with its printed lesson material reached 8,000 families, and a Bible school opened in the basement of the Calgary church in 1927 was regularly turning out new preachers.

When Aberhart became premier late in 1935, he began to be criticized for injecting Social Credit propaganda into his Sunday afternoon talks. At the same time, the Baptist ministers he successively put in charge of the Calgary congregations balked at his orders and

[33]*Calgary Herald*, July 17, 1929.

[34]This figure was supplied by station CFCN, a 10,000-watt station that carries into Montana, British Columbia, and Saskatchewan. It is likely that not more than 65 per cent of the 300,000 were Albertans.

he had four different ministers within four years. The result was temporarily disastrous. When the fourth pastor resigned in 1939, membership in the Calgary church had fallen to 40. The only advance made in these years was the organization of several small rural congregations north of Calgary. However, after Aberhart's death in 1943, Premier Manning, his protégé since 1930 and the first graduate of his Bible college, reorganized the entire Institute. Radio broadcasting was stepped up, a small monthly periodical, *The Prophetic Voice*, was printed and distributed free of charge, and the Bible school and the staff of the Institute[35] were both expanded. The new premier was careful to avoid politics in his broadcasting. By 1946 the sect had seven small town churches with a combined membership of 400, a radio Sunday school with 6,000 followers, and 500 adherents in the Calgary church.

The Westbourne people who withdrew from Aberhart's movement in 1929 became the first Alberta congregation of Regular Baptists, a fundamentalist group which Pastor T. T. Shields of Toronto led out of the Ontario and Quebec Baptist Convention in 1925. In 1933 a Bible school was opened in Calgary and soon the graduates began to build up a few congregations in rural areas. Steady expansion was shown up to 1942, when the Bible college was closed. Thereafter the sect marked time. In 1946 it had 430 members, of whom 150 were in Calgary.

Practically all the sects to start in Alberta between 1930 and 1947 were of the pentecostal variety. One of these, the Foursquare Gospel,[36] began services in Calgary in 1934, as the result of several visits paid to the city by Aimee Semple McPherson. During the late thirties the congregation lost supporters to other pentecostal groups and by 1941 it had collapsed. Meanwhile a few small congregations were opened in the Edmonton area, but by 1946 the sect's total adult membership in Alberta did not exceed 80. The doctrinally similar Apostolic Faith Mission organized a Calgary congregation in the mid-thirties which broke up early in the next decade. In 1946, it was reported[37] to have two rural congregations in the province.

Early in the thirties the first congregations of the World Alliance of Evangelical and Missionary Churches sprang up among rural Scandinavian settlements in the Edmonton area. This movement,

[35]By 1946 the staff included three clergymen and two secretaries.
[36]Cf. M. Bach, *They Have Found a Faith* (Indianapolis, 1946). Vancouver has a flourishing Foursquare church and a Foursquare (L.I.F.E.) Bible School but elsewhere in Canada the movement has not flourished.
[37]By the Alberta branch of the British and Foreign Bible Society.

reportedly the strongest pentecostal sect in Sweden, had come to this continent around the time of the First World War. In 1944 a congregation was organized in Edmonton and it opened a Bible college for the sect in 1946. By 1947 this group had nine congregations and a total adult membership of about 300.

In 1943, the Pentecostal Holiness Church, an American revivalist sect which combined pentecostal "speaking in tongues" with the holiness movement's objective of "entire sanctification," began meetings in Calgary. Beginning with 13 supporters, it grew to a membership of 58 adults by 1947, the majority coming from the Pentecostal Assemblies of Canada, the Church of the Nazarene, the Free Methodists and the Christian and Missionary Alliance. Two other small congregations were organized in the north and by 1947 total adult membership in Alberta stood close to 100.[38]

In the thirties, as in the twenties, several cults entered upon brief careers. The Liberal Catholics,[39] teaching a mixture of Roman Catholic sacramentalism and Theosophical mysticism, began in Calgary in the early years of the decade. At its peak the cult had about 50 followers, but by 1941 after losing a number of supporters to the local I Am group, it dissolved. In 1935, The Sun Movement was organized in Calgary by a few discontented followers of the schismatic AMORC Rosicrucian group. After reaching a membership of 40 in 1937, the group declined abruptly and had disappeared by 1944, although one faithful follower continued up to 1946 to rent the original meeting room and keep a lonely vigil with his Sun God. The rise of the Impersonal Life,[40] which stressed spiritual development through mental union with the Impersonal Life which created all men and controls all their acts, coincided with the shrinkage of the Sun Movement. It won supporters from this cult as well as from Unity Truth. It met for three years, attracted some 45 people and then disbanded in 1941. Some three years later a group of former members began meeting under their old leader, but without any specific cult affiliation.

The Church of Truth cult, a branch of the loosely integrated New

[38]Owing to lack of available data, no history has been provided for the following sects: the Canadian Sunday School Mission, the Church of God, Cleveland, Tennessee, the Evangelical Church of Pentecost, the Fundamental Baptists, the Gospel Missions, and the Prairie Bible Institute Missions.

[39]Cf. Ferguson, The Confusion of Tongues, pp. 278–96, and Braden, These Also Believe, pp. 318–20.

[40]One of the books published by the cult, Impersonal Life, which went through thirteen editions and sold 122,000 copies between 1914 and 1944, gives the impression that the cult advocates a form of mystic fatalism.

Thought Movement,[41] started to hold services in Calgary in 1936. Led by a woman teacher from California, it soon took some members away from the local Unity group and attracted others from various "metaphysical" home meetings. By 1938 it had secured 80 supporters. Interest waned when the original pastor left the next year, but revived under Miss Ruth Chew, who became leader in 1942. She built the membership up to 150 by 1946. In that year, she resigned and organized the Church of Divine Science, another branch of New Thought, taking with her many supporters of the Church of Truth. She did not change her doctrine, except to put additional emphasis upon popular psychology and personality development. By 1947, Divine Science was attracting 80 to 100 persons while the Truth group, under new leadership, had under 50.[42] The following of both these cults was limited to Calgary.

The Great I Am, perhaps the most quixotic of modern cults, entered Alberta in 1937. This little-known group, which originated in Chicago in 1934, was the brain-child of an itinerant salesman named Guy Ballard. In numerous books, Ballard, under the pseudonym of Godfre Ray King, described mystic experiences with "seers" and "great masters" of which Jesus and St. Germain were the most prominent. Under the personal "inspiration" of the latter, Ballard revealed the truths of salvation through ascension, reincarnation, vegetarianism, and the divine mission of the United States.[43]

The first meetings of the I Am in Calgary were organized by a telegraph operator who had brought back a copy of *Unveiled Mysteries* by Ballard from California. A group soon started in Edmonton and in both cities numerous adherents of Unity, Theosophy, and The Sun Movement became intrigued with I Am teachings. Expansion was rapid until Ballard's death in 1939 and the United States government's

[41]The New Thought outlook is summarized in *Mind Remakes the World* (New York, 1944) by New Thought leaders: "While there is a wide range of opinions among New Thought leaders . . . and laymen, this one underlying purpose runs through the entire movement: the immediate availability of God; conscious and practical application of spiritual thought force to the solution of human problems; the inevitability that good shall come to every soul; the belief in immortality and the continuity of the individual stream of consciousness and the external expansion of the individual life; the awakening not to an absorption of man's identity in Deity but to his complete unity with the whole. Thus every man becomes an individualized center of God Consciousness, eternally expanding." (Pp. 97–8.)
[42]In 1946 the new Church of Truth leader had persuaded his people to seek, for the first time, membership in the American branch of the cult.
[43]Braden, *These Also Believe*, p. 291.

subsequent conviction of his wife on a charge of using the mails to defraud. Interest revived slightly around 1945 and by 1947 the cult had about 40 adherents in Calgary and 30 in Edmonton, chiefly middle-class spinsters and widows.

Finally a cult known as the Consumers' Movement or Sound Money Economic System Movement began meeting in Calgary in 1944. Its doctrine consisted of a combination of Social Credit economics and biblical prophecy, reputedly discovered on the walls of a secret tomb in a great Egyptian pyramid. Originating in 1936 in Winnipeg, it spread across the prairies mainly through a 48-page monthly journal edited by Stuart Harris, called the *Canadian Consumer*. By 1947, this magazine had an unpaid circulation of about 23,000 copies, the bulk of which were left on doorsteps in Winnipeg, Regina, Saskatoon, Edmonton, and Calgary. Wherever the magazine's articles aroused interest, its advertising agents supplemented their soliciting by organizing study groups or congregations. "Dr." Baden, a full-time "spiritual" healer who had a lengthy association with Christian Science, Unity Truth, and The Sun Movement, organized the Calgary study group, which by 1947 had some 25 members, most of whom were formerly attached to the Sun Movement or the Hermes group. There was by this time another small congregation in Edmonton. The movement's total following in the province was under 100 persons.

ADDITIONAL NOTE ON COONEYITES. This sect was begun about the turn of the century in Ireland by Edward Cooney, originally a follower of William Weir Irvine, a Scotch preacher who was then supporting the Faith Missions in Ireland. Breaking away from Irvine, Cooney and his followers became known as the "Tramp or Go Preachers" because they always kept on the move, usually confining themselves to rural areas and small towns. Members of the sect eschewed worldly possessions and outward respectability of dress, and espoused the Jesus Way or the Lowly Way. No property was held in the sect's name, all regular meetings being held in homes. The Cooneyites have spread in some numbers to Great Britain, the United States, Australia, and Canada, and have a small following in Scandinavia and Germany. In the late twenties the Irish congregations suffered a schism, a number of the members following after a Mr. Reid, and being thereupon labelled Reidites.

CHAPTER THREE

Nature and Composition of Sects and Cults in Alberta

THE UNORTHODOX RELIGIOUS GROUPS that grew up in Alberta, although they shared characteristics which marked them off from the denominations, were of two distinct types. These have been designated by the terms sect and cult. Within each type there was considerable unity of form, in doctrine, worship pattern, organization, religiosocial protest, leadership, and membership.

Of thirty-five sects,[1] the majority were evangelical in nature, the direct spiritual heirs of separatist sects of earlier centuries, such as the Methodists, Baptists, and Congregationalists. A few, including the British Israelites, Christadelphians, Seventh Day Adventists, and Jehovah's Witnesses, were adventist in emphasis. The Plymouth Brethren and the Cooneyites were not strictly either. But corporately the groups formed a fairly homogeneous fundamentalist movement.

The doctrinal unity of the fundamentalist sects was both literal and "spiritual." They shared a tight ascetic code of morality and belief in the literal truth of the Bible, in the personal second coming of Christ, the existence of a fire and brimstone hell, and the necessity of a dramatic conversion experience. Three of the four adventist groups, the Christadelphians, Seventh Day Adventists, and Jehovah's Witnesses, rejected the idea of hell, and they and a few other sects, notably the Plymouth Brethren, the Cooneyites, and some of the older Mennonite bodies, were somewhat less emphatic about the conversion experience. With these few exceptions, the fundamentalist sects were united by wide areas of theological agreement.

The worship services of the sects also were similar. They were characterized by hearty congregational singing, "enthusiastic" preaching, long and extemporaneous prayers, and considerable lay participation. Emphasis throughout was on informality and fervency,[2] in

---

[1]For their names see Table I, p. 30.

[2]The Regular Baptists, the Swedish Evangelical Mission Covenant, the Church of Christ, the Disciples of Christ, and the Church of the Nazarenes were not consistently informal and fervent in their services, especially in urban congregations. All but the Regular Baptists, however, exhibited considerable lay participation.

sharp contrast to church worship with its stress on formality and precise dignity. Although the Christadelphians, Seventh Day Adventists, Jehovah's Witnesses, and Cooneyites were not inclined to hearty congregational singing or "enthusiastic" preaching, their services were definitely informal and fervent in tone.

Fundamentalist groups generally adhered to the congregational principle of church government.[3] This principle protected the local congregation from pressures making for formality and uniformity of teaching, worship, and week-day activity. The Salvation Army, the Christadelphians, Seventh Day Adventists, and Jehovah's Witnesses officially upheld the centralized principle of administration, but in practice most of the local branches in Alberta enjoyed considerable congregational autonomy.[4]

The sects were almost unanimous in their socio-religious protest. They bitterly attacked modernism, including all theories of evolution and biblical criticism, condemned the coldness, formality, and class-consciousness so often found in the churches, and opposed indulgence in such "worldly" pleasures as dancing and movies. In essence, their protest was against the middle class, its way of worship, its "laxity" of belief, its view of scientific knowledge, and its conventions of amusement. Fundamentalist hostility to the "world" and all institutions which were in league with it, though it varied considerably in fierceness and completeness, ran as a common motif through the pronouncements and sermons of all thirty-five sects.[5]

The leadership of the fundamentalist groups was distinctive. Sectarian leaders tended to be dogmatic and self-assured, talented in rapid verbalization and lacking in advanced education and in intellectual interests. They were commonly of humble origin and rural background.

Co-operation among the fundamentalist sects emphasized their unity. In the twenties and thirties, for instance, sects active in a particular area sometimes joined in evangelistic rallies which featured imported speakers, and during the forties, co-operation extended to the Child for Christ Crusade, the Varsity Christian Fellowship, and the Youth for Christ movement. In Calgary, most pastors of fundamentalist congregations entered a city-wide association called the Gospel

[3]Cf. W. W. Sweet, *American Culture and Religion* (Dallas, 1951), p. 84.
[4]Lately the Jehovah's Witnesses have become increasingly centralized.
[5]The Cooneyites, Jehovah's Witnesses, Seventh Day Adventists, Christadelphians, and Plymouth Brethren were perhaps most antagonistic to the "world" and usually adopt a pessimistic view of domestic politics and such international organizations as the United Nations.

Pastors' Fellowship. A number of non-denominational Bible Schools were established, whose graduates were received as pastors in about half a dozen different sects in the province.[6] Only the adventist sects, the Plymouth Brethren, and the Cooneyites took no part in these enterprises. The annual report of the Home Department of the Christian and Missionary Alliance in 1945 illustrates the sympathy that lay behind these co-operative practices:

The fraternal relations of the Society as in the past, are being maintained on a broad and sound basis. We fellowship all those of like precious faith. Our heart and hand are given to evangelical groups everywhere who contend for the faith and who make common cause against the enemies of the Cross of Christ. We commend the growth and successes of every faith movement. An increasing number of independent churches are lending support to our missionary cause. Hundreds of persons attend the great summer conventions and conferences who maintain membership in fundamental churches.

The common practice of members of fundamentalist groups in urban centres of "shopping around" from sect to sect, particularly for the Sunday evening service, was further evidence of the unity of the movement.

The fundamentalist movement in Alberta was, in many respects, an extension of that great upsurge of fundamentalism which first began around 1877 in the United States. As Garrison points out in *The March of Faith*, this diversified movement became more conspicuously self-conscious and energetic immediately after the First World War, when it sought to bring together all "fundamental" Christians and undermine the "counterfeit Christianity" of the modernists. With the exception of a few "peripheral" groups, all the sects in Alberta's fundamentalist movement were associated with this religious upheaval. It embraced as well the many thousands of Protestants in the province who, while retaining their membership in the major denominations, upheld the literal inspiration of the Scriptures and the basic evangelical doctrines favoured by the sects. In fact, Dr. Powell, United Church Superintendent of Missions for Alberta, a man who probably knew the congregations of his denomination more intimately than any other Albertan at the time, indicated to the writer that perhaps 80 per cent of the United Church membership in that province was inclined to fundamentalism. The situation was probably much the same in the Baptist, Presbyterian, and Lutheran communions. The growth in the following of the sects, however, was the clearest measure of the increase of fundamentalist strength

[6]For instance, Prairie Bible Institute supplied men to the Alliance, the Swedish Evangelical Mission Covenant, the Evangelical Free Church, and several others.

in the province. As Table I indicates their combined membership in 1946 was just over 53,000,[7] while all non-Roman Catholic denominations had about 276,000 (Table II). However, church membership lists consistently carry a good deal of "dead wood" that

TABLE I

MEMBERSHIP IN ALBERTA'S FUNDAMENTALIST SECTS, 1946[*]

Name of the sect	Membership in round figures (including children)
Apostolic Church of Pentecost	1,000
Apostolic Faith Mission	100
British Israel	200
Canadian Sunday School Mission	350
Christadelphians	150
Christian and Missionary Alliance	1,700
Christian Church, or Church of Christ	50
Church of God, Anderson, Ind.	900
Church of God, Cleveland, Tenn.	150
Church of the First Century	20
Church of the Nazarene	2,900
Cooneyites	1,500
Disciples of Christ	1,600
Evangelical Church of Pentecost	350
Evangelical Free Church of America	400
Foursquare Gospel	200
Free Methodists	470
Fundamental Baptists	350
German Baptist Church of North America	5,500
Gospel Missions	300
Holiness Movement	250
Jehovah's Witnesses	3,000
Mennonites (not including Hutterites)	8,500
Pentecostal Assemblies of Canada	5,000
Pentecostal Holiness Church	200
Plymouth Brethren, open and exclusive	500
Prairie Bible Institute Missions	700
Prophetic Baptist Church and Institute	3,000
Regular Baptists	900
Salvation Army	2,100
Seventh Day Adventists	4,900
Standard Church of America	350
Swedish Evangelical Mission Covenant	750
United Evangelical Brethren	4,800
World Alliance of Evangelical and Missionary Churches	650
Total	53,790

[*]Estimated where reliable figures were not available.

[7]This figure is only approximate since it was impossible to do more than estimate the followings of a number of the smaller sects.

TABLE II

MEMBERSHIP IN THE PROTESTANT CHURCHES IN ALBERTA, 1946*

Name of church	Total membership
Church of England in Canada	
Calgary Diocese	20,400 given
Edmonton Diocese	13,000 estimated
Athabasca Diocese	6,700 given
Qu'Appelle Diocese	1,500 estimated
Total	41,600
Baptist Union of Western Canada	10,000 estimated
Lutherans	
American Synod	
Danish Evangelical	
Augustana (Swedish)	
Evangelical (Man.)	
Norwegian	
Missouri	
Total	21,000 estimated
Moravian	2,400 estimated
Presbyterian	11,000 estimated
United Church of Canada	130,000 given**

*Since this is a table of the Protestant groups, it has deliberately excluded the Orthodox Church and the Mormons, whose combined following is in the neighbourhood of 60,000.

**This figure seems to be rather inflated, judging from other church statistics. Those acquainted with United Church methods for collecting church statistics also agree that it is rather large. A more acceptable estimate would be something between 90,000 and 100,000.

is absent from sectarian rolls. For instance one Anglican priest in Calgary confessed to the writer: "I have a total of 275 families on my roll, but only 100 of them are faithful supporters." Accordingly, the 53,000 supporters mustered by the sects in 1946 might well have been equivalent to as much as 35 per cent of the actual combined strength of the province's Protestant communions.

Expansion in Alberta's sectarian bodies occurred mainly during the First World War, the years of the Great Depression, and the Second World War. In each of these periods new sects sprang up and those already established tended to grow rapidly. On the other hand these years were generally full of strain and difficulty for the churches. All the major Protestant denominations, with the exception of the

Lutheran churches, retrenched their operations, particularly in the smaller rural villages, and suffered a decline in rural support.

The strength of the fundamentalist sects lay in the extent of their rural support. In a province whose population was at least 60 per cent rural, more than 80 per cent of the following of the Cooneyites, Seventh Day Adventists, and Jehovah's Witnesses, and more than 60 per cent of that of the Mennonites, the German Baptists, the United Evangelical Church, the Church of God, Anderson, Ind., the Pentecostal Assemblies of Canada, and many smaller bodies, was rural. Membership in the Christian and Missionary Alliance seemed to be roughly in the same ratio of rural to urban as the province's population, while that of eight groups, the Disciples of Christ, the Plymouth Brethren, the Church of the First Century, the Nazarenes, the Apostolic Church of Pentecost, the Church of Christ, and the Regular and the Prophetic Baptists, whose combined following was less than 9,000 persons in 1946, was slightly less than 60 per cent rural. In contrast, the membership of the major Protestant denominations, according to the census, ranged between 45 and 55 per cent rural, except for that of the Lutheran Church which was 78 per cent.

Some of the smaller sects tended to concentrate in a particular area. In 1946 most of the support of the Standard Church of America was found some 60 miles north of Edmonton and that of the Evangelical Free Church in a region 40 or 50 miles east and northeast of Lethbridge. Rural following was often strongest close to the town where the group had its Bible school: the Nazarenes were strong around Red Deer, and the Seventh Day Adventists around Lacombe. The larger fundamentalist sects usually had a more scattered following, the Christian and Missionary Alliance, for instance, enjoying considerable support in the central area of the province, in the district north of Edmonton, and also in villages on the fringe of agricultural settlement. In the main, the rural following of the fundamentalist movement was in central Alberta between Edmonton and Calgary, and in the more recently settled districts north and northwest and northeast of Edmonton. In other regions, such as east of Drumheller and north of Medicine Hat, fundamentalist congregations were mainly in the larger villages and towns.

The location of sectarian places of worship in Calgary and Edmonton provides a clue to the type of urban support secured by the fundamentalist movement. Only a few sects placed their buildings in the working-class districts, and these were mainly small sects like the Free Methodists, the Standard Church of America, and the

Holiness Movement. The more important groups tended to locate either downtown or within the boarding-house area. In each case, location operated to select the social strata giving support to the sect. Those sects located in the working-class districts won most of their following from their immediate neighbourhoods; those located downtown, such as the Prophetic Baptists, the Pentecostal Assemblies of Canada, and the Plymouth Brethren, drew support from every part of the city; while those located in the boarding-house area, such as, in Calgary, the Church of the Nazarene and the Christian and Missionary Alliance, were able to appeal to footloose boarders and to lower-middle-class families. Most of the non-Anglo-Saxon sects, such as the German Baptists, the Seventh Day Adventists, the United Evangelical Brethren, and the Church of God, Anderson, Ind., placed their buildings within the "foreign" belt from which they obtained the greatest part of their support. Altogether, out of the twenty-three fundamentalist sects in Calgary in 1946, eight were located downtown, five in the working-class belt, three in the boarding-house district, three in the new-Canadian section, and four in or near middle-class residential areas.

The fundamentalist sects drew supporters from every one of the main Protestant churches, and some from even the Orthodox and Roman Catholic communions. The latter two bodies lost members principally to the Jehovah's Witnesses and various pentecostal groups. A substantial number of sectarians came out of the Methodist, Baptist, and United churches, and the Norwegian and German Lutheran synods. A smaller number belonged originally to the Presbyterian Church, the Augustana (Swedish) Lutheran Synod, the Salvation Army, and the older and more orthodox Mennonite bodies. Anglican losses to the fundamentalists were apparently slight. Conversions to sects followed certain general patterns: German Lutherans tended to join German-speaking sects, such as the German Baptists, the United Evangelical Brethren, or German-speaking branches of the Pentecostal Assemblies of Canada and the Church of God, Anderson, Ind.; Swedish Lutherans affiliated with the Swedish Evangelical Mission Covenant or the World Alliance of Evangelical and Missionary Churches; Lutherans of other synods linked themselves with such groups as the Cooneyites, the Seventh Day Adventists, the Evangelical Free Church, the Christian and Missionary Alliance, the Pentecostal Assemblies of Canada, and the Apostolic Church of Pentecost; Baptists turned to the Seventh Day Adventists, the Regular and the Prophetic Baptists, and the Plymouth Brethren;

people of Methodist or of United Church background favoured the Nazarenes, the Christian and Missionary Alliance, the Pentecostal Assemblies of Canada, and the Disciples of Christ, while some found their way into the Prophetic Baptist Institute; Presbyterians went to the Regular or the Prophetic Baptists or to the Plymouth Brethren, or in some cases the Christian and Missionary Alliance; Salvation Army supporters and Mennonites usually joined the Nazarenes and the Alliance. In general, shifts in religious conviction followed lines of least ethnic, religious, and social resistance: new Canadians attached themselves to sects composed of their own ethnic group and to those English-speaking groups such as the Alliance which enthusiastically welcomed non-Anglo-Saxons; Union Baptists and Presbyterians, early conditioned to a Calvinist theological ethos, readily drifted into Calvinist groups such as the Regular Baptists or the missions of the Prairie Bible Institute. Many others of an evangelical Protestant heritage, for instance, Methodists, Congregationalists, or members of the Salvation Army, tended to turn to movements which emphasized a subjective evangelicalism—the United Evangelical Brethren, the Alliance, and the various pentecostal bodies.

Anglo-Saxon converts to the sects seem to have been people from the American Mid-West, the Maritimes, or Ontario, regions well steeped in an evangelical and sectarian tradition by 1900. Settlers who came directly from the British Isles generally showed little interest in the sects. Although the earliest English-speaking sects in Alberta, such as the Salvation Army, the Free Methodists, and the Holiness Movements, attracted few non-Anglo-Saxons, this was not true of the groups which emerged after 1920. Movements such as the Pentecostal Assemblies of Canada, the Alliance, and the Apostolic Church of Pentecost welcomed new Canadians, and by 1946 they had many members of German and Scandinavian ancestry.[8] In 1941, of the Seventh Day Adventists, 40 per cent were German or Ukrainian and another 10 per cent Scandinavian, and of the Jehovah's Witnesses, 21 per cent were Scandinavian, 9 per cent German, and 5 per cent Ukrainian.[9] A number of sects, notably the Church of God (Anderson,

[8]In the absence of satisfactory census or sect statistics on racial heritage, the writer relied on interviews with sect leaders, questionnaires answered by Bible school principals, and an examination of names in Bible school yearbooks. Thirty-five per cent of the Alliance Bible School students in one year were of non-Anglo-Saxon origin.

[9]Cf. Dominion Bureau of Statistics, *Eighth Census of Canada, 1941.* It is doubtful if these statistics, gathered while the Witnesses were banned, correctly indicate the amount of Ukrainian support the Witnesses had.

Ind.), the Evangelical Free Church, the German Baptists, and the World Alliance of Evangelical and Missionary Churches, embraced a majority of non-Anglo-Saxons, particularly people of German and Scandinavian ancestry. Still other sects such as the United Evangelical Brethren and the Mennonites had practically 100 per cent German-speaking membership. By 1946, close to 60 per cent of the 53,000 fundamentalists in Alberta were of non-Anglo-Saxon origin, more than half of these being of German ancestry.[10] The only Protestant denomination to have many non-Anglo-Saxon members was the United Church of Canada, and even in this body there were few non-Anglo-Saxon clergy.[11]

Alberta's sectarians probably fell slightly below the province's general level of schooling. The percentage of fundamentalists to finish public school, as well as the proportion to complete three to four years of high school, seems to have been low in comparison with the population generally. The entrance requirement set for fundamentalist Bible schools in Alberta up until the early forties was generally only a grade eight education.[12] Persistent opposition by sectarian groups to the teaching of evolution in the province's high schools indicates that the fundamentalist movement was untouched by secondary education and its scientific outlook.[13] Indeed, some groups, for example the Prairie Bible Institute and the Jehovah's Witnesses, were quite venomous in their attack upon modern education.

In the course of this study, various forms of investigation were undertaken in order to ascertain the economic position of Alberta's fundamentalists. At scores of fundamentalist meetings and services, sectarians were carefully scrutinized as to dress and general appearance, type of cars owned, characteristic ways of speech, and distinctive folk-ways. Heads of a number of families in four different ecological areas of Calgary were interviewed. A detailed economic

[10]The strength of the Mennonites, German Baptists, and Evangelical United Brethren was the reason for this predominance of German-speaking sectarians.

[11]The various Lutheran synods are not included in this observation. According to the 1941 census, 126,685 adherents of the United Church across Canada, or about 6 per cent, were of German, Scandinavian, and Ukrainian extraction. It is doubtful if the Alberta percentage was any higher than 6 per cent.

[12]By 1947, however, the Prairie Bible Institute, and the schools of the Nazarenes, the Christian and Missionary Alliance, and the Disciples of Christ raised their standards for entrance to grade eleven, with the proviso that exceptions could be arranged. At the same time, most of these schools established departments which provided high school instruction. Most of the other Bible schools still maintained the earlier entrance requirement.

[13]When some Bible schools began to teach up to grade eleven they demanded textbooks in biology which did not support the theory of evolution.

analysis of the membership of several small representative sects was also made. Clergy of both the sects and the churches made thoughtful judgments on the economic status of sectarian groups with which they were well acquainted. Answers to specific questions on the economic position of sectarians were received from over two hundred prairie clergy of the Anglican and United churches. Over thirty Bible school principals of prairie colleges answered similar questions. The implications of the ecological analysis of sect meeting-places in Calgary and Edmonton constituted another source of data.

It appeared that, as a group, sectarians in rural areas were usually slightly less economically secure than the majority of their neighbours. In hard times, they were somewhat more needy than the rest, and in good times, they failed to attain to the prevailing level of prosperity. There were, however, some notable exceptions, particularly among the followers of the German Baptist, Plymouth Brethren, Nazarene, Mennonite, and Cooneyite groups. On the other hand, Jehovah's Witnesses constituted an especially depressed and hard-hit group.

The great majority of urban sectarians were also of low economic status. Although, by the early forties, certain urban sect congregations, notably the Nazarenes, Disciples of Christ, Regular Baptists, and Plymouth Brethren, boasted a small percentage of members with well-paid office and executive positions, most urban fundamentalists were artisans, small storekeepers, lower-paid office workers, or general labourers. Few were factory workers.[14]

In neither city nor country were Alberta's fundamentalists generally found among the extremely poor, although a few small congregations, and certain members of other congregations, were probably very under-privileged economically. The movement seems to have found support among people of average working-class income in the cities, and slightly less than average farm income in the rural areas.

It does not follow that the fundamentalists as a body could be classified adequately as lower class. Social status is not so simply determined. Numerous observers in the province understandably ascribed to them a "low" social position, without attempting a more discriminating judgment. Certain facts already noted—the strength of non-Anglo-Saxon elements, the below-average educational attainments, the ascetic attitude to amusements, including such common foci of social life in town and country as dancing and card playing—when

[14]Owing to the limited amount of industrial activity in Alberta, it is impossible to draw generalized conclusions from this fact. Of the staff of forty in a small Calgary factory, only one worker belonged to a sect; the great majority were New Canadians, and belonged to the Catholic, Orthodox, and Lutheran churches.

combined with the complete indifference of sectarians to political questions inevitably implied an anomalous social position. Largely working class in economic standing, sectarians refused to participate in communal activities as typical members of that class. The inevitable conclusion is that fundamentalists, on the whole, were only partially integrated into the communal social structure. They constituted marginal or interstitial social strata, socially unassimilated by either the middle class or the working class. In a tightly integrated social structure, their position would be quite uneasy, but in the loosely knit communal structure of Alberta, it was not especially strained or anomalous.

The ten cults which took root in Alberta between 1910 and 1946 fell into two subdivisions. Five concentrated on spiritual healing, namely Christian Science, Unity Truth, the Church of Truth, Divine Science, and Spiritualism,[15] and were popularly labelled "metaphysical" movements.[16] Their characteristic belief was that mental (hence metaphysical) activities, consisting mainly of affirmations of and prayers for health and well-being could mobilize divine powers to ward off or cure all kinds of illness. The other five, Rosicrucianism, Theosophy, the Church of the New Jerusalem, the I Am, and the Consumers' Movement, might be classified as occult, esoteric, or mystical. They "claim to be in possession of, or to have access to, truth that is unknown to ordinary mortals but which can be revealed by various processes."[17] In general, their practice was to combine elements of Hindu philosophy with certain teachings of Christianity. But all ten cults shared an impressive area of agreement.

Alberta's cults exhibited an eclectic or syncretic approach to matters of doctrine. They combined particular ideas and teachings from Christian or occidental belief with insights from Eastern philosophy or religion, and, in the case of healing groups, with elementary truths or half-truths of modern psychology. Thus Christian Science borrowed heavily from Emerson's transcendentalism "which was a combination of the Kantian philosophy of idealism with elements of Hindu phil-

[15]Originally concerned only with communication with the dead, Spiritualism has lately embraced a strong interest in healing. Cf. C. S. Braden, *These Also Believe* (New York, 1949), p. 353.

[16]Most of them stemmed from Phineas B. Quimby, a late-nineteenth-century mesmerist and hypnotist. Mrs. Eddy, founder of Christian Science, and Warren F. Evans, Swedenborgian minister, who laid the foundations of the New Thought movement, were one-time patients of Quimby. Cf. H. L. Friess and H. W. Schneider, *Religion in Various Cultures* (New York, 1932), p. 479.

[17]E. T. Clark, *Small Sects in America* (Nashville, Tenn., 1937), p. 234. These groups are considered by some Christian scholars as ideological descendants of gnostic cults which flourished in the Near East in the third and fourth centuries.

osophy."[18] J. W. Teener listed the more apparent sources of Unity's thought as New England transcendentalism, Christian Science, Hinduism, Theosophy, Rosicrucianism, Spiritualism, New Thought, popular science, and the Bible.[19]

The cults attacked, directly or indirectly, all conventional and dogmatic religion, that is, both orthodox and fundamentalist Christianity. Those which referred to the Bible ridiculed the literal interpretations of fundamentalist groups and treated Scriptural statements allegorically or mystically. Christian Science explicitly denied the traditional Christian doctrine on sin and matter. Theosophy opposed "every form of dogmatic theology, . . . as particularly pernicious."[20] The polemic of other cults varied in its range and intensity; at the lowest point in the scale were the I Am and the Consumers' Movement, which regarded Christianity with quiet, perhaps condescending toleration, the latter cult venting all its hostility on "Fourth degree Jesuitry."

Cults were largely united in favouring an oriental rather than a Christian theory of human salvation. They displayed little or no concern for the redemption of society but concentrated upon individual salvation and various ideas of reincarnation. Unlike the sectarians, they advocated no strong stand against "the world" or against evil, although some of them did favour certain ascetic practices.[21] Several healing cults proclaimed that evil is not real but simply a mental error. This interpretation of evil was associated with a rejection of the traditional belief in hell, an optimistic evaluation of human nature and human possibilities, and a cheerful view of the future. Salvation was an easy matter consisting largely of right belief and a certain mental discipline.

Cult worship, although extremely varied in details, nevertheless embodied significant similarities. The emphasis was not on congregational singing or emotional preaching but on sermons designed to persuade and convince by their logic and appeal to thought. Congregational participation was calm, orderly, and restrained. With one or two exceptions,[22] there was a minimum of ceremonial, and little imitation of traditional Christian worship. In general, services were

[18]Braden, These Also Believe, p. 189.
[19] "The Unity School of Christianity" (Ph.D. thesis, Chicago, 1939), p.11.
[20]Braden, These Also Believe, p. 228.
[21]Most of the healing groups opposed the use of alcoholic beverages and members of I Am were enjoined to forego all sexual intercourse even if married. Cf. Braden, These Also Believe, pp. 165, 210.
[22]The Christian Science service stressed established order and ritual and minimized congregational participation. The I Am service was quite ceremonial.

characterized by an atmosphere of informal interest and serious study not unlike that of a professional lecture.

There seemed to be a cult "world" quite distinct from that of the traditional churches or the fundamentalist sects. People who became dissatisfied with one cult commonly drifted around in others and eventually joined another cult group: rarely did they return to a traditional church or join a sect. Individuals who "dabbled" in Christian Science often found their way into other healing cults or into the I Am or the Consumers' Movement. Newly converted occultists frequently circulated among two or three occult groups in the same city. In Calgary, there was a pattern of shifting from Theosophy to the Rosicrucians, to Hermes or the Sun Movement, and thence to the I Am. Incorrigible drifters were nicknamed "metaphysical tramps." Whereas changes in affiliation from healing to occult cults were not uncommon, drifting in the other direction was less usual.

Alberta's cults up until 1946 had a relatively small following. Except for Christian Science and Unity Truth, their membership was insignificant. Five of them had slightly fewer than a hundred adult supporters in the whole province. The total strength of the ten groups in 1946, as shown in Table III, was not more than 3,500. What growth there was had taken place largely during the First World War, the depression, and the Second World War.

TABLE III
ESTIMATED FOLLOWING OF CULTS IN ALBERTA, 1946

Name of group	
Christian Science	1,800
Church of New Jerusalem	50
Church of Truth (Calgary)	45
Consumers' Movement	50
Divine Science	100
I Am	70
Rosicrucians	100
Spiritualism	200
Theosophy	70
Unity Truth	1,000
	3,485°

°This figure refers mainly to adults.

Membership was concentrated in the urban areas of the province, except for a few supporters of Christian Science,[23] Unity Truth, and

[23]The 1941 census gives the Christian Scientists 583 rural followers in Alberta out of a total of 1733. The only meetings were in Calgary, Edmonton, Medicine Hat, Lethbridge, Drumheller, and Banff.

the Church of New Jerusalem. There were no cult congregations in villages or small towns. Meeting places were usually located in either the downtown or middle-class residential areas of Calgary or Edmonton.

Owning as broad a variety of religious backgrounds as the fundamentalists, cultists differed in commonly being intellectual critics of the churches and eager to discover some new slant on religion. As a group, they were people with more formal schooling than the average of the population; occultists, in particular, were avid readers, intensely interested in books on the weird and the bizarre.[24]

Anglo-Saxons predominated among cult supporters. The majority migrated to Alberta from eastern Canada, the eastern sections of the United States, and the British Isles. A significant number of occultists had come directly from the Old Country. The only important group of non-Anglo-Saxons were people of German stock, most of whom had long forgotten their European background.

The number and influence of women in cult groups was notable. Women outnumbered men in most cults to a greater extent than in the churches. The sex ratio in healing movements varied from 2:1 in Christian Science to 6:1 in such groups as Divine Science.[25] It was less unbalanced in most occult groups. Many of the women were middle-aged, and either unmarried or widowed. In the healing groups a significant number were school teachers. Cult leaders were often females, a phenomenon virtually unknown in traditional or sectarian bodies. Christian Science, Divine Science, and Theosophy were founded by women and the leader of the I Am movement since the early forties had been Mrs. Ballard, the wife of its founder. In at least seven of the ten cults in Alberta, local units were led by women,[26] and in Christian Science, women were co-leaders with men.[27]

Female predominance was coupled with a comparative scarcity of family groups at cult meetings and services. With the exception of Christian Science and the Church of the New Jerusalem, a very

[24]Field workers who went into the homes of cult members invariably discovered a number of serious books scattered about.

[25]These ratios are derived from observations at Sunday services. According to the 1941 census, 56 per cent of Christian Scientists in Alberta were women. The census and other official figures, since they embrace the children of cult families, do not indicate the true preponderance of women members. At some services of New Thought groups, the ratio was 12:1.

[26]These are Unity Truth, Church of Truth, Divine Science, Theosophy, I Am, Rosicrucianism, and Spiritualism. Moreover, "by far the largest number of mediums are women." Braden, *These Also Believe*, p. 330.

[27]The great majority of Christian Science practitioners are women.

high percentage of cult members attended as individuals. It was quite uncommon for husband and wife to show an equal interest in a cult, or for parents and children to sit together at a service.

It would appear from all the available evidence that an unusually large proportion of cultists, male and female, were inclined to neurosis and neurasthenia.[28] The proportion appeared higher among the healing than the occult groups; menopausal stresses probably loomed large among a membership weighted in the direction of middle-aged, sexually inactive women.[29] One New Thought follower told a field worker that her "church" enabled her and her friends to carry on with their deadly daily tasks, and gave people courage to face seemingly insurmountable obstacles especially "during the difficult period of middle age and the change of life."

The economic position of cult followers in Alberta might be characterized as "comfortable." Supporters of Christian Science, Divine Science, and the Church of Truth commonly belonged to the middle income brackets. One Calgary Christian Scientist told the writer: "On the whole we are prosperous people. A few come in poor but soon become prosperous. Our church includes some of the most prominent business men in town."[30] A smaller proportion of the occultists enjoyed prosperity. Perhaps half earned average incomes as bookkeepers, office clerks, or artisans. In the over-all cult movement, however, a middle-class economic level prevailed.

This financial status did not always convey general middle-class social position. Standard middle-class attitudes of condescension or suspicion confronted most known adherents of the cults. The insistence of many cults upon certain ascetic practices, such as abstinence from tobacco and liquor, tended to restrict cultists from full social acceptance in middle-class society. Life histories and interviews also revealed that a number of these people had not achieved the usual neighbourhood or community attachments of the middle class. Tendencies towards excessive residential mobility and a high proportion of single, unattached supporters accounted for this fact. In spite of "comfortable" means, accordingly, it appears that a signifi-

---

[28]Many students consider that cultists are inclined to neurosis and neurasthenia; cf. H. Laski, *The American Democracy* (New York, 1948), p. 291; L. R. Steiner, *Where Do People Take Their Troubles* (Cambridge, Mass., 1945), p. 138; G. G. Atkins, *Modern Cults and Religious Movements* (New York, 1923), p. 197. Observations in Alberta appear to confirm this.

[29]See E. Weise and D. S. English, *Psychosomatic Medicine* (Philadelphia, 1943), p. 32.

[30]See W. E. Garrison, *The March of Faith* (New York, 1933).

cant proportion of cult supporters were poorly integrated into the middle-class community. In some cases, membership in a cult seems to have represented an attempt to acquire the financial position or the social connections for acceptability. In other cases, the cult was apparently a social haven for individuals of middle-class income and outlook who, for want of satisfactory personal or family adjustments, were unable to win general middle-class acceptance. Altogether a substantial although indeterminate number of Alberta's cultists were clearly marginal to the middle-class community, while a smaller proportion composed mainly of the occult followers, were on the upper fringe of the working class.

CHAPTER FOUR

Liturgy and Doctrine: Their Role in Sect and Cult Expansion

BOTH THE FORMS OF WORSHIP and the doctrines of the sects and cults distinguished them from the denominations. Each played a part in attracting and in holding members. Thus a study of the religious and social practices which made up their Sunday worship services and an examination of their theological beliefs may throw light on the growth in Alberta of these two types of religious movement.

Among the sects, although there were many minor variations, there was a general pattern of worship not unlike that of the revivalist rallies of the nineteenth century. The nature of the pattern is indicated in the following field report:

The first hymn was "There shall be showers of Blessings"; the congregation of 110 sang with vigour, good singing with harmony accompanied by the piano and by the preacher playing the trombone. The second preacher led in the singing and clapped in tempo. The second hymn, "I know whom I have believed," was also enthusiastically and well sung. The preacher, Brother Ness, played a trombone solo after which the congregation sang "At Calvary." The preacher led in prayer for a child whose mother died last week and prayed for the sick; the second preacher and the members of the congregation constantly said "Hallelujah," "Amen," and "Glory be to God," during the prayer. Then the preacher announced the coming of a musical group at the next Sunday's meeting. The second preacher left and the first one played another trombone solo, which was quite good. He then had the congregation move into front pews and shake hands with their neighbours. Another hymn, "Do you wonder people are envious when they see how happy we are," was sung and the congregation clapped in tempo. Since this was a new hymn and not known by most of the people, the preacher instructed them to sing it again and do better, which they did. The preacher asked to see the raised hands of the people who had attended the church's summer camp; then a show of hands of those who wished they had attended camp. He then asked for six testimonials from people who had gone to the camp meeting and five women and one man gave a simple sentence in which they stated their gratefulness for the opportunity, e.g., "I'm grateful to know that Jesus lives within me." Two more hymns followed, "Wonderful is my Redeemer," and "God answers prayers." Then the preacher sang a solo, "I know a marvellous book."

In the sermon, the preacher quoted from the Bible, "Be not drunk with wine," but be drunk with the fire that is inspired by the baptism of the Holy Ghost. He said, "Cold water is refreshing but hot water generates steam which in turn generates power. People should be on fire with ecstasy through knowing Jesus."

He told a story of a salesman who is not convinced about his product and therefore cannot sell it. He quoted from the Bible (Corinthians, 12) and said, "Drink in the spirit of God and harness the torrents the way the Niagara Falls torrents are harnessed and made to generate power." He gave a short prayer asking the Lord to bless the congregation. He used every dramatic trick in the book, speaking softly and then in crescendo and shouting, and the congregation responded with many Amens and Hallelujah's.

A hymn, "He will fill our hearts with gladness," was sung and the congregation marched downstairs for the prayer meeting and Bible study.

The typical sect service exhibited an air of informality, enthusiasm, and evangelical concern. The preacher laboured energetically to "loosen up" the congregation, promote an atmosphere of spontaneous enthusiasm, and generate a sense of the urgency of individual salvation. As a rule various members of the congregation willingly participated in little rituals that guaranteed the informality and liveliness of the service. Not every sectarian service was as clearly informal and enthusiastic as the one reported above but practically all exemplified a similar spirit and emphasis. The only important exception was the Jehovah's Witnesses whose Sunday "meetings" inclined to a precise routine and a carefully restrained enthusiasm.

The principal emphases of the typical fundamentalist service were the result of certain common practices. An informal atmosphere was created by the preacher's manner of handling the service, particularly by his jokes and chatty announcements.[1] He was like a good host striving to make his guests feel relaxed and at home. Each member of the congregation seemed actively interested in the service and in all the other members. The regular members commonly extended a warm and hearty welcome to vistors, greeting them with a "Hello, what is your name? Where do you live? We hope you'll come again."

Liveliness and enthusiasm were the result of hearty congregational singing, fervent praying, emotional preaching, and congregational participation and self-expression. The words and rhythm of hymns like "All my burdens are rolled away," "Heavenly sunshine," "I thank thee for saving my soul," and "There's power in the blood," were calculated to release feelings and stir emotions. Jazzed-up tunes were often introduced to put extra life into the singing. Prayers were extemporaneous, loud, long, and fervent. The preacher poured out his feelings and the people in the congregation voiced their approval with cries of "Amen," "Yes, Lord," or "Hallelujah." The sermon was simple in language, unconcerned with rules of grammar, dramatic, fluent, dogmatic, and repetitive, and was frequently interrupted by

[1]A Salvation Army major opened a service one warm summer night by saying, "Well, I guess it's pretty hot tonight . . . and we won't need to get warmed up."

shouts from the listeners. In many sects members of the congregation prayed, testified, sang, or played musical instruments, and made anouncements or amended those made by the preacher. Certain sects, such as the Plymouth Brethren, the Church of Christ, and the Cooneyites, even allowed members to take turns in leading in prayer and sometimes in giving the sermon. Jehovah's Witnesses were encouraged to take part in the question and answer period of their meetings, and were periodically required to give doctrinal talks before their local unit.[2] Such participation was frequent, often lively, and always informal.

An evangelical focus was ensured by the type of hymns sung, by the preacher's manner of praying and preaching, and by the custom of an altar call. The hymns were concerned with sin, salvation, and the glories of the hereafter for the individual soul. The aim of the preacher was the unveiling of sin in the human heart, and the proclamation of redemption through the blood of Christ. Prayers were often little more than thinly disguised sermonettes. An altar call at the close of the sermon, in which sinners were urged to come publicly to the Mercy Seat and receive salvation, was so common among the sects as to be almost a badge of evangelicalism.

Each of the three emphases of fundamentalist worship probably played a part in attracting members. The informality and friendliness of services, which accorded with social patterns prevalent in rural Alberta, especially in newly settled areas, may have accounted for some of the sects' appeal to farmers as well as to highly mobile urban people and non-Anglo-Saxons, eager for new friends and for social acceptance. The enthusiasm and liveliness of the services, giving the impression that "those people really enjoy their religion," made them attractive to many who, through poverty, isolation, or puritanism, led dull lives. Sect services functioned like the movies as an institutionalized form of escape. Hearty lay participation in the services fitted in with the democratic semi-egalitarian social views inherited from frontier days and was welcomed by people, such as new immigrants, who could otherwise secure little recognition. Thus, sectarian encouragement of instrumental music provided people of average musical talent with important opportunities for gaining social prestige, as well as brightening up the service itself.

Fundamentalist emphasis upon evangelistic preaching and the regular altar call were also attractive to various segments of Alberta's population. Settlers of Baptist, Methodist, and Lutheran backgrounds

[2]Cf. H. H. Stroup, *The Jehovah's Witnesses* (New York, 1945), pp. 33–4.

who wandered into fundamentalist services after experiencing a period of modernist preaching often found that fervent revivalist sermons aroused pleasant emotional stirrings. Old sentiments and symbols were reanimated. To people whose ties with their denominational church had become weak, the appeal of these sermons was sometimes enough to effect a shift in religious affiliation. The presence of large numbers of evangelistically conditioned Baptists, Methodists, and Lutherans in Alberta's population, coupled with the pronounced trend toward dispassionate, "intellectual" sermons within the denominations after 1920, created a situation favourable to this fundamentalist emphasis. This was particularly so in the more rural and frontier areas of the province, where the lower educational and intellectual standards and the unsophisticated manner of living of the population made "enthusiastic" sermons more acceptable.

Again, to people of evangelical and puritan upbringing, who kept aloof from such refreshing social activities as dancing, card playing, and movies, emotional preaching coupled with evangelical hymns and enraptured praying served to provide an "emotional massage." They often experienced a stirring and release of spirit that temporarily led to a sensation of inner purification, peace, and quiet. Feelings of guilt and anxiety were momentarily discharged. The whole process was stimulating and exciting. This was perhaps most true in frontier and isolated rural communities where existing outlets for evangelical people were often drastically limited in number. Moreover, the regular altar call at services provided among other things a ceremony whereby enthusiastic converts could publicly announce their new convictions and look for social acceptance into the sect community. This religious practice offered lonely and marginal people a simple way of certifying their "belonging" to a tight-knit group.

Certain characteristics of evangelistic preaching were adaptive, too, to the outlook of the lower classes in Alberta. Its simplicity of style and unconcern for the niceties of English grammar[3] fitted in with the way of thinking and talking of unsophisticated people, particularly poorly educated farmers and city workers and recent immigrants from European lands. Its repetitiousness was similarly suited to the intellectual level of these social groups. Even the fluency and speed of delivery may be considered as socially adaptive, inasmuch as

---

[3]Even William Aberhart frequently made errors in grammar in his sermons though he was a high school principal. Some observers believe that this was deliberately calculated to win working-class support.

rural and uneducated groups, conscious of their own comparative inarticulateness, and isolated from an environment of fast, slick talkers, tend to be impressed by men capable of very rapid speech.

The effectiveness of fundamentalist worship was partly dependent upon certain patterns in the social organization of Alberta. The frontier heritage of informal and neighbourly social relations, and the presence in the province of large numbers of evangelically reared Protestants, many of whom lived at a good distance from the services of their professed church, favoured an informal, "enthusiastic" type of religious service. High rates of population movement and a large new-Canadian group inevitably implied substantial numbers of socially marginal and isolated people. Economic crises, particularly that of the thirties, accentuated the incidence of social marginality in the province and deepened the demand for socially integrative institutions. Fundamentalist emphasis upon lay participation in worship and strong in-group bonds meant that the worship patterns of the sects in some measure came to grips with these widespread social needs.

The significance of fundamentalist worship procedures for sectarian advance in Alberta was closely related to liturgical practices common to the non-Roman churches. From 1910 to 1946, Orthodox, Anglican, and Lutheran worship services retained their conventional characteristics of formality and stiffness while in the other non-Roman denominations the trend was strongly toward modernism and liturgical formalism. These churches in general failed to adjust their worship to the pattern of Alberta's social life and to the needs of unsettled groups in the rural areas, and indirectly opened the door to sectarian competitors.

The history of the Orthodox Church in Alberta, with one interesting exception, exhibits no significant effort to modify age-old liturgical practices to meet changing social conditions. Before the First World War, Russian Orthodox priests evinced a minimum of evangelical or missionary zeal in Alberta; they concentrated mainly upon carrying out the ancient liturgy to the best of their ability. Even after the split in the church in 1918 and the formation of the Ukrainian Orthodox communion the only important liturgical modification was the reduction in the length of some of the special—and very lengthy—services. The one important exception to the rigidity of Orthodox liturgy occurred with the organization of an independent Greek Church in 1905. Behind this development stood the Presbyterian

Church.[4] The new Greek Church, with Ukrainian priests and ex-purgated Orthodox liturgy, was intended to meet the needs of dis-contented Russian and Ukrainian settlers in the prairies and to hasten their assimilation. But in 1913 when nearly all its priests voted to join the Presbyterian Church the majority of the members refused to take the same step. Within a few years there were only half a dozen congregations left and the project collapsed.

In Alberta, as elsewhere, the Anglican Church failed to adapt liturgical practices to changing social conditions. Until 1914, the presence of numerous High Church clergy, sent out from England under the Archbishop's Western Canada Fund, meant that the Prayer Book liturgy was staunchly upheld. In some cases, clergy even went beyond the specifications of the Prayer Book in ornateness and cere-monial. One observer wrote:

It is a thousand pities that the clergy of the Church could not take a Plain Prayer Book stand and give a simple service to the people instead of continually worrying them over ornaments and useless accessories but they would not and as a result the Church is punished by the loss of her people. The plain people wanted a plain simple gospel without a lot of novel additions and if they could not get it in the Church they went to others who would give it to them.[5]

Although most of these High Church priests left and a relatively new group predominated between 1915 and 1925 it was still not uncommon for High Church priests to attempt to force their liturgical preferences upon Low Church congregations. Between 1920 and 1945 only a few Anglican priests attempted to modify the Prayer Book service to meet local conditions. There was virtually no recognition of the need for livelier hymns, a more informal kind of service,[6] or more evangelical preaching. A careful examination of the records of the Diocese of Calgary from 1924 to 1946 failed to uncover one single reference to the need for a different type of service. The prevailing Anglican practice was to give the people the Prayer Book service, and a teach-ing sermon. One Calgary priest informed the writer that he preached sermons to make people think: "This is probably one reason why

[4]The Manitoba College of the Presbyterian Church gave the rebellious Uniat priests who led this new church some courses in theology as early as 1905.

[5]B. P. Ingham and C. L. Burrows, *Sketches in Western Canada* (London, 1913), p. 118.

[6]A reference to the need for "altered forms of service for mission fields," in the *Report of the Field Commissioners to the Anglican National Commission*, May 8, 1941, p. 72, was, like many other suggestions in the report, largely ignored, except for a slight move toward a modified Low Church Service made by a few priests in the Diocese of Athabaska which covers an area north of Edmonton and largely coincides with the Peace River district.

my church is not jammed," he added. Liturgical inflexibility and
lack of evangelical fervour in the clergy were usually coupled with
the absence of friendliness among the congregations. It was generally
difficult for newcomers to "break into" the Church of England in
Canada. One clergyman admitted:

Each organization has its settled pattern, its settled rotation system for the various
offices, and a newcomer presents a real problem. "How shall he be fitted in?"
Our inflexible set-up probably is due to the long period of time over which it has
run without much modification. Our old-timers tend to have an unconscious resent-
ment against newcomers because they may upset the established routine.

The stiffness and formality of Anglican worship was also reflected
in the unenthusiastic and uninspiring manner in which congregational
responses were given in the liturgy of Matins, Evensong, or Holy
Communion. Altogether, Anglican worship in Alberta was lacking
in precisely those features of enthusiasm, informality, evangelicalism,
and friendliness which contributed to the success of fundamentalist
services.

In large measure the Lutheran Church in Alberta displayed a
similar insensitivity to needs for liturgical modification. Two exceptions were the Missouri (German) Synod and the Norwegian Synod,
which, having their roots in the American mid-west had managed to
preserve in worship and evangelical emphasis many of the early
lessons from their not so distant frontier past. (Significantly enough,
these two Synods expanded more than their brethren in Alberta.)
Most of the Lutheran Synods exhibited little flexibility in worship
practices and preaching. The Augustana (Swedish) group which
brought Swedish-born pastors to man the new parishes suffered a
temporary decline after 1920, owing partly to the liturgical stiffness
of these immigrant clergy. It was not until the denomination secured
a number of American mid-western and Canadian prairie clergy that
liturgical rigidities were moderated. One of these, the Rev. L. C.
Tengbom, instituted at his Calgary church in the mid-forties an
informal evening service featuring an evangelical address and hearty
congregational singing, which quickly boosted attendance. The fact
that such liturgical adaptations were rare in Tengbom's Synod from
1920 to 1940 is one reason for its slow advance in those years.

The Danish Evangelical Lutheran Synod exhibited similar rigidities,
and for the same kind of reasons. As late as 1945,[7] the Danish
Lutherans were largely dependent upon American-born pastors, and
these men, reared in a settled denominational structure, possessed

[7]Only two out of seven clergy were native-born Canadians in 1946.

little evangelical fervour. In addition, the work in Alberta failed to become independent of American direction and financial support and accordingly carried out American denominational policy including the maintenance of the liturgy in its full purity. These factors contributed significantly to a large loss of adherents, a development that had earlier occurred to this Synod in the United States.

Two German Lutheran Synods, the American Lutheran and the Evangelical Synod of Manitoba, likewise failed to modify worship procedures. Close ties with their American headquarters, where ecclesiasticism was highly developed, operated against liturgical changes in Alberta. Moreover, the respect and authority accorded the ministers, following accepted German tradition, sheltered them from influences of everyday life and made them unaware of the need for evangelical emphasis and liturgical modifications.

Even before Union the Methodist form of worship in Alberta was becoming stiffer and more formal, especially in city churches, and evangelical preaching was declining. In 1914 ministers were urged not to forget the "need to invite direct conversions at the end of the evening service,"[8] and numerous "urging" resolutions at each Conference from then on showed that spontaneity, lively congregational singing, and evangelical preaching were becoming less common. A questionnaire, sent out in 1922 by the Secretary of the Alberta Conference, Rev T. A. Moore, to a large number of Methodist ministers, asked: "Are special evangelistic services a thing of the past in your district?" A typical answer was that of Rev. W. H. Irwin of Wetaskawin: "Yes; now we have educational evangelism carried on through the Sunday School and the appeal to parents through the Sunday School."

Once Union was consummated the trend away from a warm, informal, evangelistic type of service was accelerated. Leading United Church officials have stated to the writer that Methodist fervour was cooled in adjusting to Presbyterian practices. The urge towards respectability, modernism, physical expansion, and material success also hastened the death of Methodism's evangelistic spirit. The United Church service became formal, dignified, uninspiring, and middle class in appeal. A Nazarene, a former member of the United Church of Canada, expressed her attitude to this development as follows: "They [the United Church] are so cold they just freeze you up; they don't seem to believe in having any emotion or fun in their religion." In the later thirties and early forties, some United Church leaders favoured a return to more evangelistic preaching,[9] but nothing was accomplished.

[8]*Minutes of the Methodist Conference of Alberta, 1914* (Toronto, 1914), p. 31.

By 1946, United Church worship had completely lost the evangelical features of Methodism. A Saskatchewan United Church clergyman, in response to a questionnaire concerning sectarian success in the prairies wrote:

During recent years I heard one of our ministers commence an address on "Evangelism" by confessing that he didn't know much about it. Another publicly scoffed at conversion; another got to the place in his address where the logical word to use was "converted" and he paused and added, "I won't use that word." I have told you these things because I am afraid they are representative of a very prevalent attitude on the part of our ministers.

When Presbyterianism returned to Alberta after 1930, it introduced its conventional liturgical pattern, and accordingly attracted only the "old guard" of Scotch Presbyterians. In subsequent years no significant modifications were made.

After 1920 Union Baptist services, especially in the cities and larger towns, tended to become increasingly more formal and dignified, and to copy the liturgy of the United Church. In 1935 they adopted, with slight modifications, the United Church hymnary, and a Baptist and a United Church committee co-operated in the revision of Sunday school material. Evangelical rallies declined greatly in number, and interest among the clergy turned in the direction of intellectual sermons. Thus, with few exceptions, the services of the Union Baptists by 1946 had become formal, dignified, respectable and orderly.

The liturgical formalism which characterized services of the denominations after 1930 was not an accidental development. It was a pattern of worship functionally integrated with the outlook of the dominant culture group in the province, that is, the urban middle classes and the better-class farmers and villagers. This influential social group favoured a form of service which accorded with their rigid emotional self-discipline, their pretensions to sophistication and respectability, and their level of formal education. The formalized and intellectually respectable services of the main churches (with the exception of the Orthodox communion) were well adapted to the social needs of this class. The adjustment of these denominations to the outlook of the middle classes, however, implied an incapacity to meet the social needs of the urban working class and the poorer

[9]Dean King of United College, Winnipeg, wrote: "Because the small sects carry the emotional element to bizarre extremes, we have almost gone to the length of ruling out emotion from religion altogether . . . and in our reaction to unrestrained emotionalism have made religion a cold and intellectual thing [for some people]. . . . Because it [emotional preaching] served the spiritual needs of some it perhaps ought to be retained, if only for a few." *The Sects in Manitoba,* a report based upon questionnaires to Manitoba United Church clergy (Winnipeg, 1939), p. 4.

farmers. The services of the churches thus inevitably differed from those of the sects because they spoke to different social "worlds."

Further understanding of the advance of fundamentalism in Alberta issues from an examination of the central beliefs and doctrines of this movement. To judge from the theological doctrines expressed or implicit in the regular sermons, prayers, and hymns of Sunday worship, a wide area of theological agreement bound together most of the thirty-five sects in Alberta.[10] The differences of belief which officially separated these groups were usually very superficial. For example, even the sharp contrast between Calvinist and Arminian theology, supposedly a fundamental dividing line between various sects, was seldom recognizable at their worship services, as preachers from these extreme wings of the fundamentalist movement presented apparently similar beliefs to their congregations. The main exceptions to this general uniformity of doctrine were certain beliefs of the Adventists, beliefs which exerted their own unique appeal and which will be separately examined wherever necessary to the general exposition.

The major doctrines upon which fundamentalist groups showed agreement in their worship service were as follows:

(a) All men are sinners and are guilty of deliberately flouting God's laws; they have no power of themselves to overcome sin, and without belief in the atoning work of Christ would go to hell.[11]

(b) They are saved through faith in the substitutionary death of Christ. This death wipes out the guilt.

(c) Through the resurrection of Christ, there is assurance of everlasting life.

(d) Faith in Christ comes as an experience of conversion, which is a dramatic experience of inner melting and of self-surrender to the Almighty; conversion gives assurance of salvation.

(e) Faith in Christ rests upon faith in the Bible as a standard of truth and conduct; it is the final and literal authority for religious truth and living.

[10]The Free Methodists, Nazarenes, Standard Church of America, and Holiness Movement admitted their doctrine was practically identical; similarly there was no doctrinal quarrel between the Church of Christ and the Disciples of Christ, or between the Apostolic Church of Pentecost and the World Alliance of Missionary and Evangelical Churches.

[11]The three Adventist groups, Christadelphians, the Seventh Day Adventists, and the Jehovah's Witnesses, all refused to accept the belief in hell. In fact they won a certain amount of support by their emphatic denial of this doctrine. For the most part they accepted the other doctrines without much question.

(*f*) In the Bible there are important prophecies of events to come and especially of the second coming of Christ.

(*g*) Acceptance of Christ as Saviour involves a new way of living; its marks are denunciation of the world, including the worldly churches, and worldly pleasures and lusts such as drinking, smoking, theatre-going, and card-playing.

(*h*) In one's daily life, one must depend upon God for guidance and through prayer and moral effort stay close to him.

The effectiveness of these doctrinal beliefs in assisting fundamentalist expansion was related to the degree to which modernist emphases dominated preaching in the Alberta churches after 1925. In this period, the Methodists, the Methodist-dominated United Church, the Union Baptists, the Presbyterians, and certain Lutheran Synods came to accept, in large measure, the modernist approach to orthodox Christian doctrine. (The Augustana Synod remained opposed to modernism and weeded out young clergy who upheld such heretical opinions by means of a doctrinal test at ordination; the Missouri Synod Lutherans were strict fundamentalists.) Modernism first emerged in Canada as the result of new teaching in church seminaries after 1920. The occurrence of Church Union in 1925, and the subsequent requirement by most of the Protestant denominations that theological students should have a university education, prepared the great body of seminarians to adopt a modernist outlook.[12] Perhaps because of the novelty of modernist thinking, and its close tie with the social gospel, many of the younger clergy began to preach these new doctrines with more zeal than tact, few apparently realizing how strange they sounded to the majority of Protestant church-goers. Dr. T. Hart, United Church Missionary Superintendent for Alberta in 1946, admitted to the writer that many United Church preachers felt they had to defend their modernism from the pulpit and in so doing preached a lot of intellectual sermons that "went over the heads" of their congregations. This practice was also fairly common after 1930 among Baptists and Presbyterians.

The swing to modernism affected sermons and prayers in Alberta churches in several ways: it shifted the emphasis from personal salvation and a conversion experience to social problems, social salvation, and the establishment of the Kinglom of God on earth;[13] it weakened belief in human sinfulness, and hence in the need for redemption through the Cross; it denied the literal infallibility of the

[12]While it was the United Church that first required a B.A. for theological training, the Presbyterians and Baptists soon followed suit.
[13]Cf. A. Brady, *Canada* (Toronto, 1932), pp. 129–31.

Bible and ridiculed fundamentalist biblical prophecy; it shifted attention from heaven and eternal security to a concern for making this life as secure and heaven-like as possible. Wherever taught, it was usually coupled with a lessening of asceticism; Methodists and Baptists who previously had frowned on dancing, smoking, and movie-going, had generally relaxed, by 1946, all serious restraints upon such amusements.

Substantial numbers of regular church supporters became discontented with such relaxing of puritan moral standards and with the modernist type of sermon. They were especially disconcerted by the "whittling away" of the authority of the Bible, the new emphasis upon social sins, and a this-worldly rather than other-worldly orientation. Deep-seated religious sentiments and accepted sacred symbols were apparently being questioned or criticized. These developments sometimes strained the loyalties of the older church adherents to the point of breaking. In general, they created a situation in which the more puritan and evangelistically minded church supporters were especially susceptible to influences facilitating a break with their traditional denominational group. This was noticeably true in the United and Baptist churches and in certain Lutheran churches.[14]

Fundamentalist sects launched a bitter and at times violent attack upon modernism. Modernists were accused of watering down orthodox doctrines of the Atonement and undermining the authority of morality and the Bible, thus taking away from Christians in an hour of great need just those supports that could least afford to be weakened. As late as 1947, an evangelical leader, Principal Maxwell of Three Hills, wrote in Prairie Bible Institute's *Prairie Overcomer*:

In the March issue of Reader's Digest is an article by Harry Emerson Fosdick which is typical of the man. He has always been able to use terms with two meanings. He is mystifying and illusive, double-minded and contradictory. He can tear the Bible to shreds one minute, and in the next hold it up as the Book of books. He can snatch away the Christ of Scripture in the "coldest steel of cynicism" and then with great unction (?) claim allegiance for "another Jesus" which will bow strong men in worshipful adoration. In one breath he can mutilate the orthodox faith with a vengeance, and in the next he will turn and appeal for a deeper, nobler, and more intensive devotion to the great verities (?) of the Christian faith. In this recent article he speaks of "conversion" and of being born again, but all is on a natural basis akin to a psychological experience. The psychiatrist understands him. He admits, "It has a biological (??) background." In fact Mr. Fosdick says, "I am strong for psychiatry. Sometimes I think that were I not a minister I would be a psychiatrist." This modernist is without doubt the triumphant expression of last-day religion, "Having a form of godliness, but denying the power thereof."[15]

[14]The principal Lutheran groups so affected were the Danish and Swedish Synods.

[15]April, 1947, pp. 102–3. See also May, 1946, pp. 68–9.

Such criticism helped to make many conservative and older church-goers suspicious of modernists. A division began to develop not unlike that between "High" and "Low" church in the Church of England. Led by Aberhart after 1930, the controversy was especially bitter in the rural and small-town communities of the central part of the province, an area strongly evangelical and puritan in its religious background. In some cases the denominations lost whole congregations to fundamentalist preachers. Rural congregations of the Union Baptists were particularly disturbed and a few refused to accept McMaster (modernist) trained ordinands asssigned to them by the Mission Board. This controversy was an important factor in the expansion of such groups as Aberhart's Prophetic Baptists, the Nazarenes, the Pentecostal Assemblies of Canada, and the Prairie Bible Institute.

Particular emphases of fundamentalist doctrine also contributed to the expansion of various sects or of the movement as a whole. Repudiation of many activities popularly associated with urban and middle-class living, such as movie-going and card-playing, tended to capitalize on the antipathy of rural people toward town and city dwellers,[16] and of lower-class people toward the middle class. The repudiation was most extreme among the Jehovah's Witnesses, who even supported protest parades designed to express hostility against townspeople,[17] and also among the Seventh Day Adventists, and may have played a part in the appeal of these two sects for especially underprivileged and disadvantaged people, including Ukrainian Canadians. The Seventh Day Adventists in addition forbade their Bible school students to smoke, drink, dance, play cards, go to the movies, listen to modern music, read novels, or, in the case of girls, use cosmetics or wear jewellry "other than a simple pin and a wrist-watch."[18] The Jehovah's Witnesses denounced the United Nations, civil governments, commerce, the celebration of Christmas,[19] and all the established churches.[20]

These various denunciations furnished a social outlet for the free-floating aggression common among disadvantaged groups conscious of their lack of privileges. They also functioned to devalue just those institutions and groups which tend to suppress the underprivileged, and, by reversing accepted standards and values, they conferred a

[16]Cf. J. Burnet, *Next-Year Country* (Toronto, 1951), pp. 68 ff.
[17]Several of these parades marched into Leduc in the early forties.
[18]*Calendar of the Canadian Junior College, 1944-45*, p. 19.
[19]Cf. Stroup, *The Jehovah's Witnesses*, p. 141.
[20]"At present Satan is overreaching every religious institution except that of the Jehovah's Witnesses. All present-day religion is a snare." J. Russell, *Studies in the Scriptures* (n.p., n.d.), II, p. 279.

religious superiority upon those who were accustomed to both a socially inferior ranking and an entrenched habit of self-depreciation. In Alberta, these violent protests met the social needs of the desperately poor and socially isolated, particularly members of ethnic groups like the Ukrainians, who generally met widespread social discrimination. The thoroughgoing attack of the Jehovah's Witnesses upon organized churches was well calculated to appeal to those who had become disillusioned with certain developments in the churches; it made a particularly strong appeal to numbers of Orthodox, Uniat, and Roman Catholic supporters disaffected by the mercenary, unsympathetic, or autocratic behaviour of their clergy. Among the Ukrainians this disaffection was partly related to the type of Russian Orthodox clergy sent to Canada in the years before the First World War, to the bitter clerical struggles of 1917–18 which preceded the formation of the Ukrainian Orthodox Church, and, during the depression, to the failure of some Roman Catholic priests to give sympathetic help to the poor and their withdrawal by the hierarchy from parishes in remote frontier districts. The strong core of discontent which developed among a certain number of Ukrainians and other European immigrants in Alberta played into the hands of sects like the Jehovah's Witnesses.

It is interesting that in the case of the Jehovah's Witnesses, the Seventh Day Adventists, and the Christadelphians the struggle against organized religion embraced a repudiation of the traditional Christian teaching about the existence of hell. In its place was put the teaching about the Armageddon and the erection of God's Kingdom upon the earth. It is impossible to gauge the effect of the denial of hell upon membership recruitment, although interviews suggest that this teaching did attract certain people.

Fundamentalist's emphasis upon the authority and reliability of the Christian Scriptures carried weight with large numbers of Protestants in Alberta. It especially appealed to those who had received biblical training in their youth. To people disturbed by doubts, it offered a strong support to moral and doctrinal beliefs. During the periods of two World Wars and the depression such people were numerous in Alberta, as elsewhere. Among all the sects respect and love for the Scriptures was fostered by Bible study classes, frequent references to Holy Writ during the Sunday services,[21] and the liberal sprinkling

[21]The Cooneyites and Christadelphians made Bible study the focus of their Sunday service. Each member brought his Bible and participated in scriptural analysis. Sectarian pastors would quote fifteen to twenty-five scriptural verses from memory in one sermon.

of sermons with biblical texts, but it remained for William Aberhart to capitalize most directly and efficiently upon respect for the authority of the Bible. It was his practice when preaching to hold a Bible in one hand, and, after asking some leading religious questions, to say "Well, let's see what the Bible says about this," whereupon he would leaf it over in full view of the audience, find the desired chapter and verse, and read aloud the answer to his question. Biblical prophecies of eventual victory in the two World Wars or an end to the depression contributed to rapid expansion of the Seventh Day Adventists and the Jehovah's Witnesses during the First World War, and helped the Witnesses, the British Israelites, and Aberhart's Prophetic Baptists during the thirties. Observers of Premier Manning's ministrations at the Prophetic Baptist Church in Edmonton in the mid-forties reported that he switched to prophetic sermons when attendance dropped.

The failure of prophecies apparently mattered little. In 1937 Manning forecast the coming of the Lord within a year, and asserted that the present era preceding "the last days" was fulfilling Bible prophecy by swerving away from democracy; the end of the period would be climaxed by "the collapse of democracy" and the rise of autocratic power, combined with the characteristics which climaxed the termination of five previous eras: "World wide deception, social and moral degeneracy, centralization of power, worldliness and despising of God's provenance." "Surely," Manning continued, "it can't be much longer now before the Lord himself must descend from Heaven. This is what I say may take place within the coming year. The stage is so completely set that surely it can't be left longer."[22] Aberhart is quoted as making a shadowy prophecy in June 1940 that Hitler would not invade the British Isles but would turn his back on them and "suddenly disappear," and that, if Italy came into the war, it would be on Britain's side, "although that may seem incredible."[23] When the Jehovah's Witnesses' prophecy of Armageddon's beginning in 1914 was not realized, new dates were discovered.[24]

The belief in a special divine mission which animated the Witnesses and other Adventists also seems to have appealed to certain disadvantaged sections of the population. A leader of one Witness congregation, when interviewed, said that before becoming a Witness he "felt life to be a bitter pill." Another Witness with a mixed Greek and Roman Catholic background confided: "I tried the Communists

[22]Report of an address by E. C. Manning at the Edmonton Prophetic Bible Conference, *Calgary Herald*, Sept. 27, 1937.
[23]*Calgary Herald*, June 2, 1940.
[24]Cf. C. W. Ferguson, *The Confusion of Tongues* (New York, 1928), p. 75.

for a while but I didn't like their fight doctrine. Now I have found peace of mind." The special divine mission, to which both Adventists and Witnesses felt called, provided them with a sharp sense of importance. The more socially depressed such people were, the greater their need for a bright millenial hope. It was not accidental that the Witnesses and Seventh Day Adventists had a larger proportion of the very poor and the socially objectionable in their membership than other sects in the province. Certain paranoic tendencies often associated with extreme social isolation were observable among a sizable percentage of the Jehovah's Witnesses and may help explain the stimulus which government persecution gave to the movement during the Second World War. Numerous Witnesses were arrested in Alberta during this period, but this only attracted more members to the sect.[25]

Sectarian doctrines were important to the expansion of the fundamentalist movement owing to certain peculiarities in the community structure of Alberta. The numbers of the evangelistically conditioned, the prevailing low level of education, the preponderance of the rural population, and the recency of the frontier tradition all facilitated the acceptance of fundamentalist teachings. The emergence of the modernist movement in the churches may be regarded as an attempt to impose a mature theology upon a theologically unadvanced population, with results favourable to fundamentalist groups. Conditions of social isolation common up to 1925 and still existing in certain outlying districts in 1946 favoured those teachings and sects which came to grips with the needs of the lonely and the isolated. The continuous social unsettlement that characterized Alberta's history from 1906 to 1946, especially during the two World Wars and the Great Depression also implied a crisis situation favourable to conservative, traditionalist, religious teachings which upheld the recognized symbols of authority, and promised security and stability.

Among the cults as among the sects there existed considerable uniformity in form of worship, although the occult services varied more than those of the healing cults. One New Thought service in Calgary was described as follows in a field report:

While the group was getting seated, an elderly woman played a bit of Tschaikowsky, and after Miss Chew (the leader) took her place on the platform the group sang two hymns, "Rock of ages, truth Divine," and "Sweet hour of prayer." Miss Chew began with announcements; she said that she would have office hours

---

[25]The sect increased its following in Calgary from 65 to over 125 between 1937 and 1946.

daily between 2 and 5 p.m. There was to be a meeting the next night to discuss a new location for the church, since she (Miss Chew) was being evicted. . . . After the announcements the group repeated "I rejoice in the power of Good," twice. Miss Chew requested that people turn in their vacation envelopes because during the past month the church's income had ceased. (This was a service in late August.) The group then said "Divine love," three times and the offering was taken. A great many one and five dollar bills appeared on the plate. Miss Chew announced that she had just returned from the International New Thought Alliance conference in Milwaukee and stated that she would summarize the highlights of the conference. Among the speakers in Milwaukee was Ernest Wilson, editor of the Los Angeles magazine called Progress for Unity. She said that he was a small, sunburned, genial man with a winning smile. . . . Another speaker at the conference was Louise Newman, who said "It's great to be human! Every person should have an ideal and climb up to it. Identify yourself with the inner mind of God and keep saying I know and I know that I know. You can't press clothes with a cold iron; there must be a contact with power to be effective." Dr. Myers, another speaker said that people think that all they have to do is look at Christ and they will be healed forever. Actually the power is within us and God in embryo is within each of us. Therefore we should refrain from setting up negative inner forces. . . . Dr. Gregg of Toronto told the conference that healing is our birthright. Look for harmony and you will find health; an inner harmony is what we should strive for. God is the easiest thing of all to find because He is everywhere. It is easier to say the word "well" than the word "sickness." It is important to remember that our aim is to "get heaven into men rather than to get men into heaven." . . . Miss Chew ended the service with a prayer that asked for the opportunity to leave an imprint on those who follow us. The knowledge of God dwells within us, let us use it correctly. The congregation sang "I see abundance everywhere" and Miss Chew said in closing, "No vision is too great for you. Live at peace."

Miss Chew was an elderly woman with well-groomed white hair. She wore a pale blue evening gown, and a corsage of roses was pinned to her dress. She spoke quietly without emotion. She seemed to be talking to a group of friends. Her speech was fluent and her vocabulary and grammar were good. She was neither intense nor emotional; just calm and quiet. The atmosphere was relaxed and peaceful as a result of her personality. . . .

The distinguishing features of the typical healing service were an atmosphere of informality and relaxation, a superficially intellectual type of sermon, and a ritualized recital of affirmations of God's character and presence. Although Christian Science services were formal, a warm, friendly reception was accorded newcomers; in place of ritualized affirmations they used hymns with Christian Science themes.

Informality of healing cult worship was achieved by the pastor's frequent use of colloquial forms of expression, the addressing of members by their Christian names, and a disregard of formal and routine methods of procedure. A newcomer was given the impression that he was attending a friendly meeting of religious seekers rather than a solemn service of worship. The placid relaxed atmosphere was largely the result of the leader's composed manner of speaking, and, in Unity and New Thought meetings, of periodic moments of silent prayer. An impression of intellectual profundity was created by the leaders' use of such terms as metaphysics, truth, consciousness, mortal mind, transcendental, omnipresence, unfoldment, and psychic.[26] A rather obscure kind of prose was also featured in cult writing. The following paragraph is from a Christian Science lecture delivered in Calgary in 1943:

> Man, the real man, necessarily receives from divine consciousness its contents of ideas, or spiritual, infinite, eternal facts. Then because man is the very expression of God, he necessarily expresses these ideas. That is the way God is expressed. That, then, is the perfect concept of business—unlimited reception of active good and unlimited expression of active good.[27]

Occult leaders also employed an esoteric vocabulary, including some of the words used in the healing cults and others such as aura, vibration, transmigration, guru, and hermetic.

The most distinctive and perhaps most influential feature of Sunday services in certain cults was the congregational recital of "affirmations." At one Unity Truth service the following affirmations were made:

> We are made by our kindly, heavenly Father [said once].
> We give thanks [repeated twice at three points in the service].
> The spirit of truth quickens our consciousness as we need [repeated three times].
> The meditations of my heart are of God and of the truth of which I am a part [once].
> God be merciful to me, a sinner [repeated six times].
> We bless our indwelling divinity [once].
> The white life abundantly prospers this Truth Centre and me [this was said before the collection was taken—a total of nine times].
> Our words are spirit and they are truth. They shall not be returned to us void, but shall accomplish that whereunto they are sent at once [once].

The affirmations in the Calgary branch, though less numerous, followed the same pattern. They included such phrases as "I rejoice in the power of God and in the power of good."[28] Each person repeated these "affirmations" slowly and in a loud clear voice, accenting strongly the important words and maintaining throughout a serious, deliberate

[26]Harold Laski refers to the language of the Christian Science textbook, *Science and Health*, as "esoteric magniloquence." *The American Democracy*, p. 291.

[27]*Calgary Herald*, Oct. 19, 1943.

[28]Some of the affirmations made at the 1948 I.N.T.A. Conference at Sacramento, Cal., were: "We affirm the good. This is supreme, universal and everlasting; we affirm the divine supply. He who serves God and man in the full understanding of the law of compensation shall not lack. We affirm Heaven here and now, the life everlasting that becomes conscious immortality, and the quickened realization of the indwelling God in each soul who is making a new Heaven and a new Earth." *New Thought Bulletin*, summer, 1938, p. 20.

manner. Many were said several times, apparently to implant the basic idea more firmly in the worshipper's mind. The decrees of the I Am cult were somewhat analagous to healing cult "affirmations," but longer, rather weird, and recited in a rapid staccato manner and a harsh, demanding tone. The following were some of the decrees taught to neophytes in the I Am study groups:

In the Name, by the Power, through the Love, in the Authority and unto the Glory of the Mighty I Am Presence we now offer ourselves as a channel to YOU, Blessed Master Saint Germain, Jesus, Nada, Great Divine Director and Legions of Light! Blaze through us! Blaze through us! Blaze through us! Thy Mighty Golden Power of Divine Love and *Charge* the Energy in the Gas Belts below the Earth's Surface with that Mighty Power!

The last decree is followed by a note:

On the word "Charge" bring the hands down to your sides with dynamic energy but be perfectly relaxed. Visualise and feel GREAT COSMIC STREAMS OF GOLDEN LIGHT SUBSTANCE blazing down through you from great BEAMS above you. *This actually takes place,* streaming like an avalanche through your body, hands and feet, flooding into the gas belts below the earth's surface.[29]

The appeal of cult worship was predominantly with certain types of urbanized middle-class people, particularly women of superficial intellectual interests, who for one reason or another were not "at home" in the churches. Earnest participation in the recital of "affirmations" probably strengthened a sense of belonging, while the practice of asserting that blessings were being received instead of petitioning God for favours probably helped to bring such people into the cults. On the whole, however, these people were attracted either because they found cult services "quite stimulating mentally" or because they enjoyed "the quiet relaxing atmosphere." It was also a comfort to be among other "seekers after truth." One intelligent observer in Calgary characterized the services as "pleasant escapes" for people of dilettante tendencies. They apparently provided "safe" mental stimulus for certain middle-class people of limited intellectual achievements whose appetite for learning had been whetted by reading some popularized psychology and philosophy. The shortage of adult educational facilities in Calgary as compared to Edmonton may have accounted for the greater strength of the cults in the former city.

[29]I Am Study Group Outline (Chicago, 1938), p. 11. M. Bach *Report to Protestants* (New York, 1948), tells of hearing the following decree at an I Am service:
"Turn the darkness into day
Kill the sins of Godfre Ray [the pseudonym of leader Guy Ballard]
Manifest, manifest, manifest,
I AM, I AM, I AM."

The more important doctrines shared by the healing groups which operated in Alberta were:[30]

(a) Science and religion are a unity.

(b) The Bible contains God's truth. Its understanding requires an allegorical or spiritual form of interpretation.

(c) God is Love, Goodness, Mind. He is all powerful. He has nothing to do with evil.

(d) Evil is an error or illusion and definitely transitory.

(e) God permeates everything. His power is always and everywhere available. He is inseparable from the human soul.

(f) Prayer is the way of utilizing the inexhaustible power of God to banish every human ill.

(g) Through the discovery of divine laws that run the universe, and the use of prayer, man can attain full health, happiness, inner harmony, and prosperity.

(h) There is no hell. All men will ultimately be saved; all are immortal.

(i) Through prayer and study everyone can realize these truths, receive God's power, and become a metaphysician.

The general orientation of healing cult doctrine was adapted to the intellectual and secular values of the urban middle classes. By affirming the unity of science and religion, accepting the necessity of reinterpreting many Biblical passages, and by assuming an optimistic attitude toward evil and the after-life, it circumvented certain intellectual difficulties that beset educated and reflective people. At the same time, the retention of basic Christian concepts such as belief in the Bible, prayer, immortality, the importance of Jesus, and God's love for man, preserved sufficient elements of the old faith to suggest continuity with historic Christianity and support claims to social respectability. The acceptance of such middle-class secular values as respect for science and the importance of health, economic well-being, and social harmony recommended it to worldly minded middle-class elements. Teachings which emphasized the resources for the development of personality in prayers, meditations, readings, and "affirmations," along with the promise of practical results in healings and social harmony, were also well adapted to the utilitarian valuations emphasized in business and middle-class circles.

The attempts of the cults to attract the middle class in Alberta, however, faced serious competition from the leading denominations.

[30]This exposition is confined largely, though not exclusively, to the healing groups. Some occult groups differed significantly in doctrine.

The latter's development of a formal, dignified service fitted in well with patterns of severe emotional self-discipline and impersonality in business characteristic of the middle class. Modernist interpretations of Scripture were accommodated to middle-class respect for modern science, and professionalized standards among the clergy accorded with middle-class business standards. The relaxation of puritan restrictions also found favour with the same class. The prominence of leading business men and citizens in the top councils of the churches and the financial and material success of the denominations in the cities of Alberta, as elsewhere on the continent, were indicative of the close alignment between the denominations and the respectable middle classes.

Particular cult doctrines varied greatly in their contribution to expansion. The unity of religion and science, which was expressed in the names Christian Science[31] and Divine Science, and reiterated and expanded at cult services, was also frequently expounded by leading modernist preachers. Again, while the cults' repudiation of fundamentalism and scriptural literalism, and their allegorical interpretations of the Bible, appealed to critics of a naïve biblical literalism, so also did the modernist interpretations of the Bible set forth vigorously in many urban pulpits. Moreover, the healing cults and the denominations both emphasized the doctrines of the power and love of God.

The practical orientation of cult teachings gave a distinctive appeal to these and other doctrines. The power of God was held to be immediately available to believers and to guarantee them a vast increase in personal dynamic. Thus one of Unity's favourite "affirmations" was "The Power of God has awakened in me!"[32] The theme of God's love was so interpreted as to emphasize the importance of living in harmony and congeniality with others. It was claimed that God's love enabled people to make and keep friends. Sermons provided positive suggestions on how to become socially acceptable. Teachings on evil and suffering aimed at being highly pragmatic. It was asserted by most healing groups that God had nothing to do with evil or with punishment. At one Unity meeting in Calgary the leader expressed this as follows: "God is no more responsible for evil than the ocean is for the flotsam and jetsam that is washed up on its shore." Evil was considered not a thing in itself but simply a state

[31]Ferguson in *Confusion of Tongues* (p. 208) notes that "the very term Christian Science carries a theological wallop. It answers rather conclusively the charge of conflict between science and religion by affirming that religion is science."
[32]Bach, *Report to Protestants*, p. 197.

of lack of goodness. Both evil and suffering were viewed as impermanent and basically unreal. Such discounting of the reality of pain
and evil fostered the conviction that through "right" thinking all
psychic ills could be overcome. It attracted certain people of neurotic
leanings and seemed to fit in with current theories of psychotherapy.

The healing cult doctrine of omnipresence which blurred the distinction between God and his creatures formed the basis for attractive
teachings on prayer and human perfectibility. Since God was so close,
argued healing doctrine, mental prayer could secure anything. The
speaker at one Unity service attended by the writer outlined the
method of prayer as follows: "Prayer is like asking one's earthly
father for gifts; you affirm that you will get the gift knowing the love
of your parent, you give thanks in advance, and you *will* receive
what you pray for." Followers of Unity Truth and New Thought
were taught not to ask God for blessings but to *affirm* that the blessings
were already being received. A similar approach to prayer characterized the other healing groups. It is significant that cultists were
encouraged to seek from God such practical things as prosperity,
success, poise, happiness, and inner peace. Unity Truth especially
encouraged its followers to affirm prosperity. A typical advertisement
in their devotional magazine *The Daily Word* was: "Whether you
are seeking prosperity, a new home, a new job, health, or adjustments
of personal affairs, do this one thing. Release your problem trustingly
to God and leave the solution to Him. His answer will certainly come,
and His ideas will guide you in making right decisions."[33]

Fashions in prayers changed with conditions. Up until the late
twenties the stress was upon physical health. During the depression
prosperity was emphasized and after 1940 attention was directed to
mental health. Again, during the Second World War, divine aid was
increasingly sought on behalf of inner peace and harmony, freedom
from worry, and maturity of the personality.

The concentration of prayer upon such practical goals undoubtedly
helped to recommend the healing groups to urban and middle-class
groups. Religion became a practical way of meeting problems. In a
period when the denominations in Alberta had abandoned the traditional prayer meeting and allowed their faith in prayer and the
supernatural to become shallow and formal, the emphasis of the
healing groups on *practical* prayers was bound to be attractive. Its
new "affirmation" way of getting divine aid furnished a novel and
psychologically defensive method of saying prayers that tended to

[33]*The Daily Word* (Kansas City, Mo.), May 1946, p. 46.

interest many persons who had previously found their spiritual efforts discouragingly ineffective. Frank encouragement of prayers for mental health and development of personality undoubtedly impressed the neurotic and socially self-conscious. Prayers for prosperity appealed to the financially embarrassed and the social climbers. The attraction of the healing cults' practical approach was summed up by a member of the Calgary Church of Truth:

People today want a practical, livable religion; something they can take home from church and use in their daily life. . . . Metaphysics provides a practical help to people and makes possible the abundant life. *We are placed here on this earth to have happiness and there must be some way of getting health and prosperity.*

Unity and New Thought teachings on the utilization of spiritual laws for the attainment of human perfection were positively accommodated to the progressive outlook of middle-class people. This doctrine ascribed infinite powers of improvement to spiritually enlightened man. Particularly among the occult groups the doctrine of perfectibility embraced the goal of becoming a genuine metaphysician by the acquisition of ever greater esoteric knowledge. Private study and reading were thus encouraged, as a means not only of widening one's mental horizon but of securing exalted status in one's cult.

The opportunity which the cults offered of attaining social recognition through religious activity was largely unmatched by any specific teaching of the denominations in Alberta. It paralleled various practices among the sects but appealed to a different group, namely members of the upper working class and the lower middle class who lacked the prestige of a higher education.

In form of worship and doctrine the cults were much closer to the modernist denominations than to the sects. While the sects prospered among the large lower-class rural and urban groups of the province which the denominations to some extent had abandoned, the cults found themselves in competition with the modernist churches for the support of the relatively small number of urban middle-class city dwellers. The success they achieved was in some measure due to their extreme individualism and pragmatization of religion, their repudiation of traditional concepts like sin, evil, hell, and the wrath of God, and their confident promises of personal power and adequacy. Occult groups in particular seemed designed to interest that section of the lower middle class which prized knowledge and intellectual achievement from a distance and welcomed the opportunity to advance toward its goal through private effort and study.

CHAPTER FIVE

Characteristics of Programme and Organization in Sect and Cult

ONE OF THE CLUES to the success of the sect in frontier areas is that it tended to become a close-knit community. (Certain sects are of course absolute communities.) The social advantage of such a feature is obvious in a loosely integrated frontier society: it met the pressing human need for fellowship and solidarity "in depth." Thus a typical Christadelphian interviewed by a field worker confessed that the fellowship and brotherly love in his group were as necessary to him as bread and butter. While it is true that agreement on fundamental doctrines and attitudes contributed to such close fellowship, the weekday activities of the sect were at least of equal importance. In point of fact, certain social procedures common to most fundamentalist sects facilitated the development of a close-knit community. These practices were largely embodied in an accepted programme or routine calendar of events.

The weekly prayer meeting played an essential role in the spiritual and social cohesion of almost all local sect congregations. By no means every member habitually attended these meetings, but a high percentage did, particularly the "inner ring" and those on its fringe. The meetings varied considerably in form and content, depending on size, leadership, and zeal. Within the more evangelical groups people took turns in praying and testifying, usually to a low but audible accompaniment of "Amens" and "Hallelujahs." Pentecostal prayer meetings were oriented towards the receiving of the Holy Spirit and the speaking "in tongues," and usually involved a fantastic medley of entreaties, prayers, moans, and physical contortions.[1] Besides individual prayers and "seeking," most meetings featured enthusiastic hymn singing and an address on or discussion of some biblical topic.

The significant sociological feature of these weekly meetings was their provision for the spontaneous and uninhibited expression of deeply imbedded emotions and longings. Problems and anxieties were

[1]Cf. M. Bach, *Report to Protestants* (New York, 1948), p. 132.

brought to the Mercy Seat of God, in the presence of the brethren. On occasion, the vocalized prayers served as an excellent emotional cathartic. In addition, prayers were made for the sick, and in many groups, testimonials of faith and of joy in knowing Christ were voiced aloud. These meetings thus provided an acceptable outlet for a wide range of sentiments, anxieties, and desires, a freedom of expression which tended to foster an intense sense of unity. They also impressed new-comers, who were not disturbed by the intellectual and spiritual level of the proceedings, with the depth of the sect's unity. Accordingly they not only met social needs for communal integration, but also tended to draw into the sect lonely people who sought a sense of fellowship.

The spiritual and social value of prayer meetings was long known to church leaders, including the clergy of Alberta's main denominations. Before the First World War, Baptist and Methodist congregations in Alberta usually held weekly meetings like those the sects held in the forties. Early Presbyterian congregations also had regular prayer meetings although of a somewhat more sedate character. The disappearance or transformation of these services, first apparent in the city congregations, began in the second decade of the century. Among the Methodists, the suggestion recorded in the Minutes of the 1911 Alberta Conference that "prayer meetings be established on every appointment"[2] hints that interest in weekday meetings was already beginning to wane. An identical resolution was passed in 1914, with a rider encouraging the practice of congregational testimonials.[3] This rider was of particular significance since testimonials are the very core of a strong evangelical prayer meeting; when they disappear, the whole structure of the meeting undergoes changes. By the early twenties, in the majority of Alberta charges, the old-fashioned prayer meeting had been either dropped or replaced by a more dignified and formal service, and by 1930, five years after Union, nearly all trace of the earlier form of meeting was gone. Presbyterianism found less place for the old type of weekday meetings after the First World War, and when, after Union, it re-emerged in Alberta the meetings had lost practically all their evangelical character. With the Union Baptists the trend was somewhat delayed, but by 1940 this church's prayer meetings consisted mainly of a few hymns and a lecture or biblical address. The German Lutheran Church also failed to maintain the old-fashioned prayer services during and after the thirties, the effect of which was a loss of support, particularly among German

[2]*Minutes of the Methodist Conference of Alberta,* 1911 (Toronto, 1911), p. 44.
[3]*Ibid.,* 1914, p. 31.

migrants from Russia who had been accustomed in their homeland to strong lay control and to great informality and "enthusiasm" in their prayer meetings. Sometimes these people drifted into German-speaking sects such as the United Evangelical Brethren.[4]

The mid-week meetings of the Jehovah's Witnesses featured speeches by the members on Witness doctrines instead of singing, prayer and a sermon. The content and delivery of each speech was afterwards evaluated by one of their leaders, according to a prepared list of criteria such as pace, volume, and clarity. Comments were generally brief, but pointed and constructive. This procedure helped to train the members not only in Witness doctrine but also in English pronunciation and grammar and in public speaking, social skills which assisted directly in the vertical mobility of Anglo-Saxons and the assimilation of new Canadians. Such training may well have contributed to the success of the Jehovah's Witnesses among lower-class Anglo-Saxons and European immigrants.

The revival meeting was also common among the fundamentalist sects. This might be a one-day "stand" or a series of meetings lasting a week or more. The speakers were usually travelling evangelists imported for the occasion. In practically all of Alberta's evangelical sects, each congregation commonly promoted one or two revival meetings annually, and in certain groups, such as the Pentecostal Assemblies of Canada, the Alliance, and the Apostolic Church of Pentecost, they were held much more frequently.

Revival rallies in Alberta had developed a rather rigid pattern of organization by 1946, involving advance advertising by church announcement, press, and poster, the importation of an evangelist who was either well-known or young and dynamic, and some special musical attraction. Neglect of one or more of these items commonly spelled disappointment or actual failure.[5] The demand for dynamic travelling evangelists had become so steady and insistent, particularly among the pentecostal churches, that a systematic advance booking arrangement had grown up. Successful evangelists notified prospective "customer" congregations up to a year in advance of an intended visit to their town, and sought a definite booking for a week or more of meetings. The evangelist was thus ensured of a steady round of

[4]In Calgary from 1940 to 1946 a group of German Russians still formally attached to the Lutheran Church met regularly on Sunday afternoon and Wednesday evening for special prayer meetings, renting for the purpose an unused United Church building. The writer visited a Wednesday night meeting and found it being addressed in German by a Church of God pastor.

[5]Such was the case, for instance, with the Free Methodist and Plymouth Brethren revival rallies held in the summer of 1947 in Calgary.

preaching appointments and the interested sects of a stream of new faces and new "talent." Most of the professional evangelists came from the American middle and far West.

The revival meetings were intended to revive backsliders and convert sinners, and such was the intensity of their emotional appeal and the pressure of group expectancy that they undoubtedly did rekindle the religious fervour of some people and transform the life-pattern of others.[6] In addition, the meetings provided rural people, particularly in outlying areas, with both entertainment and emotional release. In the cities of Calgary and Edmonton they were popular with people of evangelical background and with lonely people who craved excitement and fellowship. It was no accident that numerous boarding-house residents were drawn into the fundamentalist camp through revival meetings.

Fundamentalist success with revival rallies was closely related to the abandonment of this evangelical technique by the leading Protestant denominations. Before the First World War the churches were favourable to revivals. The *Minutes of the Methodist Missionary Report,* 1910, stated: "Conference unanimously thought revival campaigns are absolutely necessary in order to grapple with the hard moral soil of many rural neighborhoods. . . . Brother Bell was set apart for two years for such work; he had missions on eleven fields in 1909 and brought in 729."[7] None the less revival campaigns gradually became unfashionable. Their neglect began among the Methodists in the early twenties and was accentuated by union with the Presbyterians and Congregationalists. During the thirties the revival meeting dropped altogether out of United Church programmes, in some congregations being replaced by lectures or discussions on social issues. The emphasis shifted from personal to social salvation. The leaders in this development included several politically active pastors associated with the Alberta School of Religion.[8] During

[6]The power of a pentecostal rally to convert even the sceptical is portrayed in Bach, *Report to Protestants,* pp. 142–3. The writer was aware on more than one occasion of the weight of collective emotion that presses upon visitors at such meetings.

[7]*Minutes of the Methodist Missionary Report for Alberta,* 1910 (Toronto, 1914), p. 45.

[8]This summer school, begun in 1925, originally attracted some 150 clergymen and laymen. During the late thirties its increasing radicalism cut support down to less than half this number. It brought such left-wing Christian leaders as Harry F. Ward and Scott Nearing from the United States to address its annual summer gatherings.

Another social gospel project was the Christian Commonwealth Youth Movement, which was led by Rev. F. Kelloway. It collapsed when he resigned, under pressure, from Knox Church, Calgary, and went to New York.

the Second World War a reaction set in and the Alberta Conference of the United Church gave more attention to the annual reports of its committee on evangelism, but up to 1946 no old-fashioned revival rallies had been organized.

The abandonment of revival services among the Union Baptists began in the twenties, because of declining interest and a dearth of effective evangelists.[9] By 1940 they had begun to substitute Evangelical Institutes and visitation evangelism. In 1944 a full-time evangelist was appointed to organize and conduct visitation evangelism programmes in interested congregations. Thus, by 1946, revival rallies were being superseded by new techniques of evangelism.

A third practice common to evangelistic sects in Alberta was the summer camp meeting. Among the sects, outdoor camp meetings, which included evangelistic services led by outstanding preachers, replaced revival meetings during the summer months. They were usually held near a lake, on a site equipped with dormitories, a tabernacle, a dining hall, and a playing field, and were timed so as to coincide with the slack period in farming. By 1946, about half of Alberta's sects were running such summer camps and attracting large numbers of followers and numerous visitors.[10] The Seventh Day Adventists had three camps and the Cooneyites five.

The camp meetings provided cheap and pleasant holidays for whole families, in the company of friends and fellow-believers. Such vacations were attractive to many people, especially during the war years when hours of work were exceptionally long. In addition, by bringing together unmarried men and women from various parts of the province, camp meetings facilitated mate selection and "endogamous" marriage, which the smallness of any one sectarian congregation often appeared to frustrate. The assembling of members of the same sect for a week or more of close association also aided the general social unification of the sect and reinforced group morale, as the following extract from the minutes of the 1945 Conference of the Church of the Nazarene in Alberta indicates:

The Camp Meeting of 1944 was in deed and in truth wonderfully blessed and owned of God. . . . Rev. Harold L. Volk and Dr. A. O. Hendricks were our

[9]Cf. *Minutes of the Western Union Baptist Conference*, 1922, p. 16.

[10]A leaflet publicizing the Nazarene camp in 1946 lists some of its attractions: "One of the finest sites for a religious summer camp in Western Canada. It is easily accessible from the business district of the progressive city of Red Deer, Alberta, and yet, lying as it does on the east side of the Waskasoo Creek, it is a secluded spot where spiritual inspiration and physical relaxation are the natural reactions. Besides the large commodious tabernacle, there is a splendid dining hall, prayer cottage, dormitories, and cottages—for everybody, with accommodation to suit every taste and pocketbook."

engaged Evangelists. Truly they were men sent from God for the occasion. Again and again the long altar was lined from end to end with earnest seekers and just as often, the tabernacle was the scene of extraordinary visitations of the Holy Spirit's presence and power. Thank God for Red Deer Camp![11]

The camps sponsored by the denominations bore little resemblance to those of the sects. Instead of serving the entire family they were usually restricted to children and young people, their programme was more educational than evangelical, and in orientation they were more individualistic than communal. These differences in programme and constituency reflected the denominations' adjustment to the norms of holidaying among the middle classes.

Prayer meetings, revival rallies, and camp meetings were regular items in the apparatus of the fundamentalist sect. Explicitly they helped distinguish it from other types of religious groups and implicitly they revealed a common evangelical outlook. They constituted media for that emotional catharsis so important to the kind of guilt-ridden personalities found in evangelical groups. They built up the sect's morale and "recharged" its emotional batteries. In frontier and strictly rural communities they contributed significantly to the sectarian role of upholding a puritan moral order and creating a community for evangelically conditioned people.

Certain common principles of organization and administration among Alberta's sects likewise contributed to their expansion. The adoption of such principles generally underlined the grass roots character of the fundamentalist movement.

One regular feature of sectarian organization was that fundamentalist congregations were normally composed of a small number of members practically all of whom were very active. With the exception of urban units of the Nazarenes, the Apostolic Church of Pentecost, and the Pentecostal Assemblies of Canada, fundamentalist congregations in Alberta rarely had more than 250 members apiece. Generally they had slightly under a hundred members in the cities and fewer than fifty in rural communities. To some extent the small size of sectarian units was the result of strict membership requirements and

[11]*Minutes of the 1945 Conference of the Alberta Church of the Nazarene* (Kansas City, Mo., 1945), p. 39. An M.A. thesis dealing with rural life in Southern Saskatchewan commented: "The religious and social life of the congregation was climaxed by the summer camp meeting. . . . People came from all over south-western Saskatchewan. . . . To the members of the church the camp meetings were nearly as important socially as religiously. . . . [They] bound the various congregations together. It was a time . . . [of] visiting . . . [when] the young people had an opportunity of meeting members of the opposite sex from other communities." B. B. Peel, "R.M. 45: The Social History of a Rural Municipality" (M.A. thesis, University of Saskatchewan, 1946), p. 296.

the belief in adult baptism. Interested adherents usually had to undergo a period of probation and show by their behaviour that they were genuinely ready for membership in the sect. The small size of sect congregations allowed the pastor to become acquainted with all his flock and to give personal attention to their psychological and spiritual needs. It made possible those personal relationships between the members that promote a strong "in-group." The fact that sectarians referred to each other as "brother" and "sister" pointed to the family-like integration of their congregations. New members entered into a close network of personal relationships which gave a lively sense of belonging.

Church congregations in Alberta commonly had a different type of organization. City congregations usually numbered from 400 to 1,000 members; Central United Church in Calgary boasted over 3,000 members in 1946. In consequence, except within certain parish organizations, which seldom embraced altogether more than 25 per cent of a congregation, formal, impersonal, and business-like relationships obtained. Pastors had little time to give to the pyschological and spiritual problems of their parishioners. Even in small-town and village congregations with their fewer members, the family-like integration of the sects did not normally prevail, partly because of leadership procedures and partly because of the predominent middle-class outlook. Especially in city congregations a new church member was just one more person and might easily drop out after a few months without being missed. Thus the denominations failed to provide the type of intimate fellowship found in the sects.

The active participation of members in the week-day programme was another important feature of sect organization. Fundamentalist groups usually had such an extensive programme, including prayer meetings, frequent revival services, and Saturday-night street-corner meetings, that the whole social life of many members was centered on the sect. The renunciation of "worldly" amusements aided this development. Continuous participation in sect activities bound the members of the local congregation into a close-knit fellowship. The Jehovah's Witnesses, which had few mid-week meetings, compensated by requiring intensive "publishing," that is, door-to-door peddling of Witness literature, or its display on busy city street corners. Since the "publishing" was usually done in teams, it also fostered group morale and integration.

The limited size and elaborate mid-week programme of fundamentalist congregations meant that there were a large number of status-giving offices to be distributed among the members. Most sectarians had an opportunity to hold one or more offices within their congregation for which religious zeal and willingness to work rather than special talent or educational achievements were the chief requirements. This was nowhere more true than in the Jehovah's Witnesses, where posts such as "service committee member" or "unit chairman" were usually distributed according to knowledge of doctrine, success in selling literature, and capacity for "speech making." The availability of these offices appealed strongly to members of the lower classes and particularly to new Canadians, insofar as religious prestige helped to compensate for deprivations in the secular world. Prestige ranking in a sect also bound the members more tightly to their local congregation. The comparative dearth of offices within denominational congregations heightened the significance of the fundamentalist procedure. Churches seldom had enough offices to involve more than 10 or 15 per cent of their members. Since, however, the majority of denominational adherents came from the middle class and enjoyed a respectable social and economic standing, this situation was not generally considered invidious.

The increasing number of young sectarians who attended fundamentalist Bible colleges after 1930, regardless of any settled intention of entering the ministry, was another significant feature of sectarian organization. During the war years more than 50 per cent of the Bible school students in Alberta were young women, the majority of whom had no original expectation of undertaking ministerial or foreign missionary work upon graduation. Some Bible colleges, including those operated by the Mennonite groups, concentrated entirely upon producing lay leaders, while others, like the Christian Training Institute of the German Baptist Church, prepared a large majority of their graduates for such work. The result was that after 1940 several hundred biblically trained young people returned annually to serve as lay leaders in their respective congregations. Their education in fundamentalist morality and doctrine and in evangelistic techniques enabled them to assume positions of leadership in the Sunday school, the prayer meeting, the youth work, or Sunday Services and even to undertake home missionary activities in areas adjacent to the local congregation. Some of these Bible school graduates actually organized Sunday schools and adult "missions" in "unchurched" districts and thus concretely assisted in the expansion of their sect. The fact that, among the leading denominations, only the Lutherans had set up similar lay training institutions in Alberta by 1946 emphasizes the strategic importance of this practice.

The adherence of evangelical sects to the principle of congregationalism also contributed to their expansion in Alberta. Some groups, such as the fundamentalist Baptists, the Church of Christ, the Disciples of Christ, and the Standard Church of America, made this principle one of their basic tenets. With others it was more a matter of operational expediency than of official policy.[12] Even in the groups which were not congregational in organization (certain Adventist groups and a few other sects, of which the Nazarenes and the Pentecostal Assemblies of Canada were the largest), centralization was seldom highly developed because of the weakness of sectarian bureaucracy and the power of prairie traditions of independence.[13] Congregationalism permitted variety in worship, congregational organization, and doctrinal emphasis. It meant that the balance of power was held by the members of the local congregation rather than the clergy or sect hierarchy. Leaders could scarcely afford to ignore suggestions made by laymen concerning the modification of worship patterns or congregational policy to meet local needs. Lacking substantial financial backing from sect headquarters, a pastor's failure to please his people often meant either a starvation salary or a return to secular employment. It was in the face of these imperatives that fundamentalist leaders experimented with such measures as radio broadcasting, the organizing of Bible schools, the holding of Saturday-night street-corner services, or the importation of leading evangelists or faith healers for special revival meetings. The result was that the sects moved with speed and success into new fields of evangelization. A congregational polity which released the local minister and congregation from the restrictions of excessive ecclesiastical conformity made it possible for them to adapt old techniques so as to take advantage of conditions peculiar to their locality. This was particularly important in Alberta owing to the constantly changing socio-economic conditions within many of its communities.

Conversely, the centralized control characteristic of the churches favoured the creation of ecclesiastical machinery which leaned toward uniformity and propriety rather than speedy adjustment to local needs. In some of the denominations, including the Methodist, United Church, Presbyterian, and, to a certain extent, the Church of England, the centre of power was in eastern Canada; in certain Lutheran groups, it was in the United States. Central church boards were thus separated from the Alberta scene both by distance and by differences in social and cultural outlook.

[12]The Plymouth Brethren sect, which had originally stressed uniformity, gradually became congregational. See H. G. Ironside, *A Historical Sketch of the Brethren Movement* (Grand Rapids, Mich., 1942), p. 134.

[13]Centralization and authoritarianism in Adventist groups are related to their stress upon religious prophecy.

The fact that the Union Baptists on the prairies were organized regionally into the Baptist Union of Western Canada and had, until 1946, only limited contacts with the All-Canada Baptist Federation, did not prevent a trend towards centralization. During the thirties central prairie boards were established, not only for Sunday school papers, but for young people's and home mission work, pensions, and social service. Increasing co-operation with other Protestant denominations in the provincial Religious Educational Council and with the Canadian Council of Churches strengthened tendencies toward uniformity. Distinctive Baptist patterns were flattened out and in particular the shift toward a liberal theology and an accommodative attitude to secular amusements was strengthened. From the early twenties until the mid-forties the use of modernist Sunday school lessons printed in the east met with bitter and persistent opposition from a number of congregations, and in 1947 one Calgary Baptist Church was still defiantly using American fundamentalist Sunday school materials. Centralizing trends in theological education led to violent clashes with certain rural congregations over the appointment of modernist seminary graduates and to the defection of numbers of evangelical-minded Baptists to fundamental bodies. At the same time, as Baptist youth came to lean upon their regional Young People's Board for direction and inspiration their interest in evangelizing neglected rural districts seemed to dry up.

In the United Church of Canada, centralization was an inevitable accompaniment of the need for uniformity on basic policy that was a by-product of Union and of the dream of a national Church increasingly held by leading United Church officials after 1940. The kind of pressure exerted upon congregations and clergy is shown by the objectives for congregations suggested in the report of the Missionary and Maintenance Committee for 1940:

We would draw the attention of every Official Board to the plan of advance for the year 1940, as outlined by the Church in Bulletin No. 4, and recommend that it be the subject of study by each and that the aims set forth in Bulletin and Poster be adopted, and every effort made to realise them, namely:
  (a) 25% increase in church attendance.
  (b) 6% increase in church membership.
  (c) 10% increase in Sunday School membership.
  (d) 16% increase in membership of Young People's Society.
  (e) 10% increase in membership of Women's Missionary Societies.
  (f) Each member engaged in definite Christian service.
  (g) Everyone a Christian steward.[14]

Pastors and congregations in rural areas often criticized such "objec-

[14]*Report of the Alberta United Church Conference*, 1940.

tives" as reflecting the urban and eastern bias of leaders at central headquarters in Toronto. Particularly in radio broadcasting and seminary education, the centralization of the United Church held back expansion in Alberta. As early as 1927 the Home Mission report of Alberta encouraged local clergy as well as the Edmonton College to engage in regular broadcasting, but it was not until 1943 that an effective radio committee began to function in Toronto, and several years later before this had much effect in Alberta. Similar delays occurred in the organization of regional Bible training institutes for lay leaders. Again, because of the powerful influence of eastern seminary leaders, an Arts degree was made the prerequisite for theological training at the time of Union, and since few young men in the West could seriously consider entering the United Church ministry in the face of this requirement, the result was a great decline in the number of recruits for the ministry in Alberta which subsequently contributed to the withdrawal of the United Church from many rural communities.

In Anglicanism, also, centralization militated again the growth of the church. Although mainly at the diocesan rather than the national level, its effect in ecclesiastical traditionalism, organizational red-tape, and the demand for rigid uniformity among the clergy led to a failure to adjust to Alberta conditions. In fact, by the forties, maintenance of the ecclesiastical machinery meant that, on the one hand, a great deal of the time of the average parish priest was absorbed in "paper" work for various diocesan committees and reports, and, on the other hand, a large proportion of the time and energy of the diocesan synod was annually expended purely upon matters of finance and canonical reform. Moreover, the procedures adopted for the election of parish wardens and lay delegates to Synod favoured the selection of elderly men of pure English stock who were strongly opposed to changes in the organizational structure of their religion.

The top-heavy ecclesiastical machinery of the Presbyterian Church affected its adaptibility in much the same way. The principle concern among continuing Presbyterians after 1925 was the re-establishment of the old ecclesiastical system and the provision of services of the traditional Presbyterian stamp for their faithful supporters. The direction of the "come-back" after Union by Eastern committees, coupled with the resurgence of demands for centralization and uniformity once the church was on its feet, led to policies unrelated to the Alberta situation. The struggle for recovery produced no imaginative or daring innovations. The main objective was the restoration of the traditional Presbyterian forms. Concentration upon this programme gradually produced a Presbyterian Church in Alberta, but not one which made a wide appeal. It was largely an ethnic church catering to people of Scottish background.

Centralization was not pronounced among Lutheran Synods in Alberta. Since the Norwegian and Missouri Synod groups had headquarters in the American middle West, the cultural gap between denominational leaders and the people of Alberta was not pronounced. Both Synods built colleges in Alberta which enrolled several hundred students annually. From the early thirties, the Missouri Synod broadcasted from Edmonton a popular radio programme known as the Lutheran Hour. The establishment of an inter-synodical Bible school at Camrose in the late thirties was further evidence of Lutheran adaptability. On the other hand, the absence of a congregational policy coupled with the traditional rigidities of the Lutheran ecclesiastical set-up led to a failure to develop an aggressive itinerant ministry to reach isolated communities and to an indifference toward ethnic groups not originally attached to Lutheran churches.

Rigidities associated with ecclesiastical centralization retarded the adjustment of the denominations to social trends in Alberta. With policy-making concentrated in the hands of eastern committees, it was inevitable that the different rates of socio-economic maturation between Ontario and Alberta should lead to misjudgments concerning effective church polity. In consequence, the churches tended to lose contact with lower class elements. On the other hand, the location of most sect headquarters in the West, coupled with their congregational policy, facilitated speedy adjustment to new conditions.

The Jehovah's Witnesses and to a lesser extent the Seventh Day Adventists were sects in which a high degree of centralization did not retard expansion. The Jehovah's Witnesses were almost unmatched among religious bodies for authoritarian centralization and uniformity.[15] The president wrote practically all the literature, controlled finances, and was personally in charge of all the full-time workers, called "Pioneers," as well as the travelling "servants" who carried on "inspections" of the local units. All "Company Servants," or leaders of local groups, were directly responsible to him. This autocratic form of organization, however, apparently helped rather than hindered expansion. This is partly explained by the fact that the sect worked out an elaborate and efficient "chain of command," and also by the fact that it provided its followers with incentives to initiative, especially in the selling of literature and winning of new members.

[15]Centralization was not affected without considerable struggle: see W. Davidson, "Jehovah's Travelling Salesmen," *Collier's*, Nov. 2, 1946, p. 75.

Moreover, the central organization spoke directly to individual members each week through sect literature, and provided all those who were prosecuted with free legal advice. The observer may note a number of parallels between this sect and the Roman Catholic Church; the rather exceptional success of the Witnesses in winning adherents from Roman Catholicism is interesting in this connection.

Certain prominent features in the typical mid-week programme of the healing groups bear a significant relationship to the success of these cults in Alberta. Week-day healing meetings were one of the main items. In Calgary, both Divine Science and Unity Truth held such meetings regularly. Miss Ruth Chew advertised hers in the Sunday mimeographed bulletin as:

Our Divine Science Clinic. Every Friday evening at 8. Instruction is given along with actual practice in demonstration. Each one is expected to work on one desire for himself until results are obtained. Regular attendance is essential. Registration is still open.

The meetings generally consisted of a period of silent meditation, the recital of a number of positive affirmations of health, and a talk regarding the cause and cure of sickness in which it was customarily asserted that sickness was entirely due to wrong thoughts and wrong emotions, such as selfishness, hardheartedness, bitterness, hate, and jealousy. This doctrine was usually drawn from the writings of New Thought authors such as Glenn Clark, Ralph Waldo Trine, and C. B. Fillmore and from the teachings of modern psychologists.[16] Depending for its success upon the educational background, therapeutic insight, and personal qualities of the leader, the healing meeting occasionally exemplified what is called by some psychiatrists "inspiration-repressive group psychotherapy."[17] At such times, by means of relaxing procedures, positive affirmations of health and self-confidence, "transference" to the leader, and encouragement through

[16]Representative Unity views on the cause and cure of sickness are: "Our ills are a result of our sins, or our failure to adjust our mind to Divine Mind. . . . When the sinning stage of mind is forgiven and the right state of mind established, man is restored to his primal natural wholeness." *Jesus Christ Heals* (Kansas City, Mo., 1944), p. 5. Moreover "every mental process is generative . . . the thought of health will produce microbes to build up healthly organisms, the thought of disease will produce microbes of disorder and destruction." *Talks on Truth* (Kansas City, Mo., 1943), p. 18. "So the fears,.the doubts, the poverty, the sin, the one thousand erroneous states of consciousness have their microbes." *Ibid.,* p. 21. "The antidote for disease germs is turn your attention to higher things. Make love alive by thinking love." *Ibid.,* p. 26.

[17]J. I. Meiers, "The Origins and Developments of Group Psycho-Therapy" in J. L. Moreno, ed., *Group Psycho-therapy: A Symposium* (New York, 1945), p. 267.

testimonials of fellow-members, people with psychosomatic disorders would be partially or fully cured. The Wednesday night testimonial meetings of Christian Science congregations were rather similar in orientation to New Thought healing meetings, and, in so far as they built up confidence in faith healing and radiated a positive, optimistic atmosphere, shared in the latter's therapeutic values.[18]

The healing meetings benefited from an extreme shortage of facilities for the treatment and cure of psychosomatic disorders in Alberta. In Calgary there was only one trained psychiatrist up until 1947, and he practised psychiatry part time. In both Calgary and Edmonton popular knowledge of the field of mental disease and psychosomatic illness lagged considerably behind that common in large eastern cities. The use of a few psychological terms was often sufficient to suggest a profound understanding of mental processes. Popular ignorance of psychiatry went along with the widespread prevalence of conditions like social marginality, culture conflict, vertical social mobility, and social isolation that are usually closely related to mental and psychosomatic disorders.

Another important part of the mid-week programme of healing groups was the study circle. In Calgary these usually met in the members' homes or in the church if the groups became too large. Miss Chew advertised the Divine Science Study Circle in her Sunday bulletin as follows:

Course for Thinkers.—Wednesday evening at 8 p.m. Strong Faith can be developed through realization of how Science backs up true religion. The union of these great factors in life form the basis of our study.

Study circles held by the Calgary Unity Truth and Church of Truth generally catered to specific groups such as business men, young people, and housewives, and met at convenient hours in each case. In 1946 there were about ten housewives' discussion circles in Calgary, some of which were not directly attached to any specific healing cult. Most of the members of these groups were middle-aged and of middle-class status. Their studies concentrated on "metaphysical" doctrine, healing procedures, and religious truth. These study circles were the smallest social unit within the healing cults and provided a warm, friendly, social atmosphere for religious inquiry. Their informality in particular facilitated the invitation of visitors and the gaining of new supporters for the cult.

No less important than the weekly meetings were the personal counselling services of cult leaders. In Unity and New Thought this

[18]Cf. L. S. Reed, *The Healing Cults* (Chicago, 1932), p. 82.

work was carried out by the minister, in Christian Science by the practitioner. The counselling was done either at the church office or in the home of the patient. It followed a simple routine: listening to the patient's story, asking questions to aid in spiritual diagnosis, and then a "treatment" consisting of prayers, "affirmations," and verbal persuasion aimed at driving out the "mental error" lying behind the complaint. This sympathetic suggestive therapy appealed to people whose psychosomatic ailments tended to receive rather abrupt handling by regular medical men. The importance of personal counselling in the cults was related to the large size of urban church congregations, which tended to prevent the clergy from giving time and attention to psychologically disturbed parishioners. This was reflected in the grievance voiced by Calgary cult members against denominational clergy who neglected to visit their people. The shortage of psychiatric facilities, coupled with the almost complete absence of clergymen with some knowledge of psychiatry, served to underline the need for people who would provide mental therapy.

The importance of healing meetings and personal counselling in promoting cult growth is suggested by the fact that occult groups, restricted in their mid-week programme to study circles, expanded much less rapidly than healing cults. It is also suggestive that Christian Science testimonial meetings, which because of their stereotyped character lacked the possibilities for group therapy of the New Thought healing meetings, failed to attract new-comers in like numbers. Through their home meetings, healing meetings, and personal counselling, the New Thought groups provided a "practical" religion adjusted to the needs of insecure middle-class people and capable of providing for them a feeling of acceptance and fellowship. The failure of other institutions to furnish such "facilities" cleared the way for the advance of New Thought.

Of the various organizational principles observable among Alberta's ten cults, two appear to have aided expansion. The first of these was the lenient attitude toward membership characteristic of all the groups except I Am and Christian Science. Unity Truth[19] simply required that new-comers sign a membership card; there was no ceremony of initiation. Many New Thought groups paid little or no attention to formal membership. The Calgary Church of Truth neglected to incorporate itself until ten years after organization, and only then required its followers to sign a membership card; some old

[19]Unity Truth "still claims categorically that it is not a church or a sect but a school." C. S. Braden, These Also Believe (New York, 1949), p. 146.

supporters disliked this new turn of events and refused to sign. New Thought, Spiritualist, and Unity Truth groups did not require that new members forswear their previous religious allegiance, and supporters of these movements in Calgary often retained some connection with an established church. Numerous cultists in Calgary approved of such an easy-going membership policy and gave interviewers the impression that they would resent the adoption of any narrow and exclusive membership regulations. This casual attitude toward membership was related to cult notions of religious tolerance, and although it retarded the establishment of an exclusive and dogmatic cult loyalty, and facilitated religious drifting, its wide appeal in the long run probably drew in new supporters.

Among cult groups the local leader commonly enjoyed a position of almost unlimited importance, except in Christian Science and I Am, both of which emphasized the cult founder and discounted the local leader. In some cults the local leader was the cult, and did nearly all the work single-handed. In Calgary, the local units of Unity,[20] New Thought, and Spiritualism were extraordinarily dependent upon their ministers or leaders and the success and vitality of each congregation hinged completely upon his or her charisma and skills. This development was the result of decentralizing trends within the cults and of the counsellor-patient relationship that tended to exist between leader and follower. Thus the cult was to quite an extent a leader-disciples fellowship. If the leader was weak, the local congregation suffered; if he was strong, it flourished. While favouring rapid expansion under a strong leader this principle naturally made for erratic advance.

In Calgary these two characteristics of cult structure operated principally to the advantage of the Divine Science group. It gained by loose membership regulations and a skilful leader at the expense of some other cults, including Unity Truth and Christian Science. The open and easy-going membership policy of New Thought groups capitalized upon the bias toward non-denominationalism common everywhere on this continent but particularly strong in areas like Alberta that were still close to the frontier stage. The very flexibility of their organizational structure, like that of their doctrine and ritual, was well adapted to the mobility and instability of prairie urban centres.

[20]In recent years the Unity Movement has moved slowly in the direction of centralization. Cf. M. Bach, *They Have Found A Faith* (Indianapolis, Ind., 1946), p. 252.

The Role of Leadership in Sect and Cult Expansion

SHORTLY AFTER the First World War there emerged on the Canadian prairies a number of sectarian educational institutions, commonly called Bible schools, whose aim was primarily to produce pastors for the fundamentalist movement. The phenomenal growth in size and number of these institutions contributed most significantly to fundamentalist expansion in Alberta and elsewhere in the Canadian West.

The Bible school was an institution which trained young people in biblical knowledge, Christian apologetics, and techniques of home missionary work. The academic course usually lasted three to four winter seasons. Unlike the theological seminary, the sectarian Bible school did not confine its student body solely to prospective ministers. Anyone who wanted to consolidate his or her knowledge of the Bible and grow in the Christian faith was welcomed. Academic hurdles and fees were generally low. Usually several courses were offered which varied in content, difficulty, and length of study required. Graduation seldom led automatically to ordination, as it does in the theological seminaries. Estimates provided by school principals indicated that about 80 per cent of the graduates in any one school normally applied for ordination, while about 15 per cent of the students failed to finish their courses.

The first Bible school on the prairies was the Prairie Bible Institute which began at Three Hills, Alberta, in 1922 and since then has gained a national reputation. During the succeeding years, as Table IV indicates, new institutions emerged almost every year. The first two, the Prairie Bible Institute and the Winnipeg Bible Institute, were non-sectarian schools whose graduates entered the ministry of the newer sects, for example the Pentecostal Assemblies of Canada and the Alliance; but most of the later schools were attached to individual sects. By 1947 there were 24 sectarian[1] and 8 non-sectarian Bible

[1]This figure includes five Mennonite schools—there may have been more than

TABLE IV

PRAIRIE BIBLE SCHOOLS

Name	Location	Denominational affiliation	Date of beginning	Number of students 1947
Prairie Bible Institute	Three Hills	Non-denominational	1921	450
Western Bible College	Winnipeg	P.A. of C.	1925	150
Winnipeg Bible Institute	Winnipeg	Non-denominational	1925	40
Canadian Nazarene College	Red Deer	Nazarene	1927	43
Christian Training Institute	Edmonton	German Baptist	1928	102
Miller Memorial Bible School	Pambrun	Non-denominational	1928	57
Calgary Prophetic Bible Institute	Calgary	Prophetic Baptist	1929	108
Church of God Bible School	Moose Jaw	Church of God (Tenn.)	early 30's	32
Moose Jaw Bible School	Moose Jaw	Free Methodist	early 30's	
Regina (Evangelical) Bible Institute	Medicine Hat	United Evangelical	early 30's	37
Saskatoon Bible College	Saskatoon	Non-denominational	1931	18
Alberta Bible College	Calgary	Disc. of Christ	1932	30
Alberta Bible Institute	Camrose	Church of God (Ind.)	1932	49
Peace River Bible Institute	Sexsmith	Non-denominational	1933	25
Bethel Bible Institute	Saskatoon	P.A. of C.	1935	135
Briercrest Bible School	Caron (erstwhile Briercrest)	Non-denominational	1935	215
Two Rivers Bible School	Carlea	Non-denominational	1935	28
Western Holiness Bible School	McCord	Holiness Movement	1936	10
Grande Prairie Bible School	Grande Prairie	Non-denominational	1940	100
Covenant Bible Institute	Prince Albert	Mission Covenant	1941	44
Western Canada Bible Institute	Regina	Alliance	1941	190
Prairie Apostolic Bible Institute	Saskatoon	Apostolic Church of Pentecost	1943	85
Full Gospel Bible Institute	Eston	Full-Gospel Missions	1944	36
Radville Christian College	Radville	Church of Christ	1945	19
Alberta Bible College	Edmonton	Apostolic	1946	15
Temple Bible Institute	Edmonton	Western Canada Alliance of Missionary and Evangelical Churches	1946	22
Can. N.W. Bible Institute	Edmonton	P.A. of C.	1947	50

colleges in the West. Alberta had 12 of the former and 3 of the latter, but graduates from all the prairie institutions often came to Alberta and served its sectarian congregations.

this—which had a simpler curriculum and shorter term than the other schools and did not graduate ministers. There were three such Mennonite colleges in Alberta in 1947. At least three other fundamentalist Bible schools existed for a time and then closed, two at Calgary and one at Wetaskawin, run by the Regular Baptists, the Pentecostal Assemblies of Canada, and the Swedish Baptists respectively.

For sect members, the schools had many appeals. They provided a place where young people of either sex could acquire theological knowledge and insight not available within the local congregation. They gave youth with doubts about the Bible or their vocation a chance to "study systematically the Word of God and prepare for some branch of Christian service."[2] They offered "an antidote to the great flood and tide of modernism and other false cults."[3] Brother Toms, a member of the staff of the Prairie Apostolic Bible Institute in Saskatoon, wrote:

> In these last perilous days, false cults, isms and ideologies abound on every hand and truth is hard to find in the avalanche of commentaries, articles and books that flood the market and scream aloud for attention. Therefore it is good for us to turn from it all to the precious word of God which from the first verse of Genesis to the closing verse of Revelations IS TRUTH. (John, 17:1). This is no doubt the reason why in the mercy and providence of God that so many bible schools true to the word of God of which P.A.B.I. is honoured to be one, are being raised up.[4]

The leaflets of the Foursquare Bible school in Vancouver, called the L.I.F.E. Bible College (Canada), set forth other reasons for attending these institutions:

> Because the Foursquare Movement offers you an unlimited future as a soul-winner. . . . Because you will associate yourself with other fine, clean-living, spiritual, companionable, agreeable young men and women. . . . Because the dominant spirit back of the College, and the motivating spirit taught by the School is world-wide Evangelism. Because the courses are all very comprehensive and yet easy of mastery by the ordinary person.[5]

The schools offered young people interested in assuming lay leadership in the sects training in organizing and speaking. They also tried "to *discover* talent for the Christian ministry."[6] They provided a situation in which youths could become acquainted with the work of the ministry, without encountering extreme pressure to adopt a ministerial career.

The constituency of the Bible schools was broadened by the fact that the fees charged were extraordinarly low. During the early forties, many schools provided tuition, room, and board for less than $4.50 a week. As late as 1946, most charged under $6.00 a week. Non-residential schools such as the Calgary Prophetic Bible Institute limited

---

[2]Article by Pastor Kyllo, *Yearbook of the Prairie Apostolic Bible School* (Saskatoon, 1947), p. 6.
[3]*Ibid.*
[4]*Ibid.*
[5]*L.I.F.E. Prospectus*, p. 8.
[6]*Covenant Bible Institute Prospectus*, p. 3.

their annual tuition fee to about $10.00. Such fees attracted numerous young people from the denominations who were unable to meet the cost of enrolling in a theological seminary. In fact, it was probably cheaper for some families to send their children to Bible school than to board them all winter at home. This may partly account for the considerable number of sisters and brothers who went to the schools at the same time.

The low fees were made possible by economical policies of administration and management. Many institutions grew their own food on school farms, did their own laundry, and printed their own pamphlets. The work was shared out among the students. The prospectus of one school stated:

Students are expected to do a certain amount of gratis work each day, which means that the girls should bring aprons, and there may be occasions when the young men will require overalls. The Lord deliver us from turning out pansies and dandies, afraid to work with their own hands.[7]

The meals served were plain. The living accommodations were unpretentious, most of the school buildings being of simple frame construction like that of prairie farmhouses, equipped with few modern conveniences, and lacking large or attractive grounds. Miller Memorial Bible Institute warned prospective students: "We do not offer as an inducement to attending here anything in the line of scenic surroundings, modern conveniences, sports, ease or worldly honor."[8] Salaries of Bible school teachers were commonly very small. Gifts of foodstuffs and money were constantly solicited from friends and neighbouring farmers.

The term of study at the schools was from late October to mid-April, coinciding exactly with the winter lull in farm work and with the period of the year when recreational and social outlets for youth were often very limited. The Bible schools offered a full programme of activities: each day included an hour or two of physical work, some hard study, corporate prayers, and recreation such as group singing and dramatics. Staff and students often took part equally enthusiastically. One teacher at the Prairie Bible Institute stated: "I have never been so happy as since I came to P.B.I. It is like one great family: we all pitch in and do our best, we share and share alike. It's a marvellous experience." Frequent revival meetings, periodic conferences, and visits of travelling evangelists added excitement. The student body in most schools was small, and homogeneous

[7]*Prospectus of Miller Memorial Bible Institute,* 1947, p.9.
[8]*Ibid.*

in cultural background, age, outlook, and dress. The simplicity of living arrangements, orderliness of routine, and strict morality tended to duplicate or to improve upon the small-town or rural life to which the students were accustomed and facilitated the organization of satisfying recreational programmes and the establishment of strong group morale.

Bible school provided rural youth with a means of escape from unattractive occupational prospects. Since young men were in short supply in many small towns, a number of young girls normally faced careers as housekeepers, teachers, and clerks, and the Bible school was a most acceptable alternative, for it offered a respectable, sheltered social environment for three years, furnished contacts with marriageable men of similar socio-economic backgrounds,[9] and provided training for missionary work. To young men who were being squeezed out of farming by increased mechanization, it opened up a ministerial career.

Bible schools, furthermore, offered rural youth a means of improving their social status. A preacher in a rural community enjoyed high social standing, regardless of his ethnic background; thus young Mennonites or Ukrainians could anticipate attaining improved social standing through Bible school training. Graduates who entered foreign missionary work, about 15 per cent of all Bible school students, could expect special recognition from sect members as well as prestige on the mission field, and even those who returned as laymen to their home congregations were often accorded high status because of their training. The Bible school's promise of increased social rank was made the more enticing by the scarcity of channels of mobility in small prairie communities; the high schools did not train their graduates for a specific profession, while technical schools and inexpensive agricultural and arts colleges were few in number.[10] In general, Bible colleges gave individuals with little schooling who were attracted to ministerial or missionary careers a chance to rise socially. Investigations of the Federal Council of Churches of Christ in America showed that in the mid-forties there were in the United

[9]Many did find husbands among the Bible school students, in spite of restrictions imposed on social intercourse. At Prairie Bible Institute and Briercrest Bible Institute the principals almost invariably refused to permit couples to become engaged during the college term. Students got around this regulation by arranging summer work in adjoining areas and becoming engaged in the summer time.

[10]Small arts colleges included Luther College, Regina (German American Lutheran Synod), Mount Royal College, Calgary (United Church), and Camrose Lutheran College (Norwegian Synod). There were agricultural colleges at Olds and Vermilion.

States over 4,000 young men interested in the ministry, most of whom had no more than one or two years of high school. Both in the United States and in Canada, the Bible schools, with their low entrance requirements, availability of general academic courses along with theological instruction, short period of study, and low fees, attracted many such people who, even if they belonged to the denominations, could not have met the academic requirements of the denominations' theological seminaries.

The young persons to whom the Bible schools offered greatest opportunities were those who spoke fluently. Bible school training often enabled such individuals to attain leadership in their sect, or to find permanent and well-paying work as travelling evangelists. In either case, they rose in the social and the economic scale. Radio evangelists like J. D. Carlson and preachers like Bentall, May, and Laing are examples.[11] In this respect, Bible schools were not unlike selling agencies in that they promised greatest success to extroverted personalities with exceptional verbal skills.

The Prairie Bible schools opened the way for geographical as well as social mobility. Young people in the smaller rural communities of the West often longed to see the world. Bible School propaganda for home and foreign missions, reaching its peak at annual missionary conferences, pointed out how they could satisfy this desire. Numerous students indicated to the writer that the stress upon adventurous service abroad was one of the most important attractions at certain schools. The drive for foreign missionaries was sometimes so intense that, as one student of Prairie Bible Institute claimed, "You feel you are hardly doing your best if you go into full-time work here in Canada!" In the last fifteen years about four hundred prairie young people have actually embarked upon missionary work, chiefly from Briercrest Bible Institute and Prairie Bible Institute; in 1947 the latter institution claimed 270 graduates in foreign mission fields. During the same period the seminaries of the denominations, except for a few Lutheran synods, enlisted only a handful of men for foreign missions.

The introduction of high school departments in some of the larger Bible colleges widened their appeal. By the early forties, high school courses were being given at Prairie Bible Institute, Briercrest Institute, Nazarene Junior College, Bethel Bible Institute, Regina Bible Institute, and the Seventh Day Adventist Canadian Junior College. At first

11In 1946 Bentall was pastor of the Edmonton Pentecostal Assemblies of Canada congregation, May of the Calgary Pentecostal Assemblies of Canada congregation, and Laing of the Calgary Prophetic Baptist Church.

their purpose was to furnish a secondary education within a fundamentalist framework and to fill gaps in the educational background of students interested in the Bible school course. Subsequently, several larger schools, including Regina Bible Institute and the Canadian Nazarene College, introduced certain secular subjects of a junior college level to take care of deficiencies in the training of their theological students made evident by experiences on foreign mission fields. In curriculum the high school departments followed the provincial requirements fairly closely, although some institutions, like the Prairie Bible Institute which still lacked an accredited rating in 1946, modified the provincial courses in English and history as well as biology.[12] Briercrest Bible College taught both the provincial textbook's approach to evolution and its own interpretation. All the schools required some Bible study in the high school course and daily attendance at chapel. By providing the accepted provincial high school curriculum within a residential school where the students were under strict supervision, the Bible schools appealed especially to farm parents whose alternative was to board out children in a high school town. Parents concerned about the moral welfare of their offspring looked on the Bible school as a "safe" boarding arrangement. Since the United Church as an economy move during the depression had closed down its two prairie secondary schools and two Women's Missionary Society Educational Institutes,[13] the new sectarian high schools frequently attracted young people from denominational homes. In such cases biblical indoctrination often imparted a fundamentalist outlook and sometimes drew these young people into the schools' theological departments.

[12]The biology text was not named in the 1947–8 calendar. For Grade x history, *Ancient History in Bible Life,* by D. R. Miller, was used. In English, the prose selections included, in Grade ix, *The Triumph of John and Betty Stam,* by Mrs. Howard Taylor; in Grade x, *Bunyan's Pilgrim's Progress;* in Grade xi, *Hudson Taylor's Spiritual Secret,* by Mrs. Howard Taylor; and in Grade xii, *The Life of Madame Guyon,* by T. C. Upham.

[13]The following resolution was recorded in the Minutes of the Alberta Conference of the United Church for 1946: "Secondary Colleges—Whereas the Secondary Colleges of the United Church have suffered seriously from the action of the General Council of 1936, when the long-standing policy of the Church was changed, and whereas many schools of the same status are generously supported by religious organizations, making it possible for them to charge much smaller rates and fees and thus appeal successfully to United Church families of moderate means, or less, therefore be it resolved that this Alberta Conference memorialize the General Council to recognize the distinctively Christian character of our Secondary Colleges and reinstate them to the important place they held prior to 1936."

Bible school leaders were aggressive in the use of radio to spread their gospel and advertise their schools. In 1946, at least thirteen fundamentalist colleges sponsored regular broadcasts, many of them an hour long. Evangelical hymns and an evangelical message, announcements about the school, appeals for financial aid, and testimonials from students made up the programmes. The broadcasts thrilled the young people who participated as well as their parents and friends, interested potential students, and brought in revenue through mailed-in contributions.

Appeals from listeners for assistance in organizing fundamentalist congregations in their local communities made it possible for the schools to open up home missions in those parts of the province inadequately served by the denominations. It was mainly through radio that the non-denominational Prairie Bible Institute and Briercrest Bible Institute became sponsors of the Fellowship of Gospel Churches and the Association of Gospel Churches. Graduates of the two schools who were unacceptable to the main sects on personal or theological grounds became leaders in these sects.

During the early forties, the larger schools found broadcasting so remunerative and effective that they took steps to increase the extent of the hook-up; Briercrest Bible Institute developed a hook-up which covered all parts of Canada, at one time including twenty-five stations. In 1946, when radio revenue had fallen off, their net annual income was still $25,000. Prairie Bible Institute in November, 1947, began preparing transcriptions of their radio services to go to CKOV, Kelowna, British Columbia, CHWK, Chilliwack, British Columbia, CKBI, Prince Albert, Saskatchewan, and CFBC, St. John, New Brunswick.

The facility of the Bible schools in initiating activities popular in rural Alberta was closely related to their freedom from hampering ecclesiastical controls and to the youthfulness and grass roots character of their leaders. The non-sectarian schools were most independent of inhibiting regulations, but the sectarian institutions usually enjoyed considerable freedom also, partly because of their experimental character and partly because of the newness and lack of centralization of the sects to which they were attached. Exceptions were the seminaries set up by such older groups as the Swedish Evangelical Mission Covenant, The Free Methodists, and the Holiness Movement, which had moved in the direction of centralization and uniformity. The average age of the principals in the prairie Bible colleges was about forty, and that of the teachers about thirty-six. A majority of both principals and teachers came from rural communities in western Canada and the western United States, and had received only the amount of schooling usual in such communities, few having reached Grade XII and some having barely passed Grade VIII. They were of varied ethnic background: principals of non-Anglo-Saxon origin included Kyllo of the Prairie Apostolic Bible School, Peterson of the Covenant Bible Institute, Magzig of the Regina Bible Institute, Hildebrand of the Briercrest Bible Institute, and Wahl of the Christian Training Institute. Several Anglo-Saxon principals had a working-class background, like Hutchinson of the Calgary Prophetic Bible Institute, Maxwell of the Prairie Bible Institute, and Thomson of the Canadian Nazarene College.

By contrast, there was a gap between the age and outlook of the staffs of western denominational seminaries and that of large sections of prairie rural youth. The predominance of grey-haired principals and middle-aged teachers in these seminaries, few of whom had much first-hand experience of prairie rural life and conditions, militated against the adoption of new or unusual procedures of promotion or student enrolment. The result was that, in accord with secular professional trends, they stressed mainly the maintenance or the elevation of scholastic standards.[14] Admittedly, high costs of seminary education, the length of study required, and the hampering restrictions of centralized denominational policy all helped to curb the growth of denominational colleges on the prairies, but the social distance between their teaching staffs and the rural masses undoubtedly aggravated the problem.

Much of the success of the Bible schools resulted from their close integration into the prairie rural social structure. This was clearly evident in such objective factors as their location and architectural design. Over 50 per cent of the schools were situated in small cities and towns and were a natural part of the rural hinterland; four schools were on the geographical frontier of Saskatchewan and Alberta. By contrast, all the denominational seminaries were in big cities. Architecturally, the Bible schools were seldom impressive in structure or equipped with many modern conveniences; their design was generally utilitarian and unpretentious. Church seminaries were big, stone structures with every modern convenience.

[14]Dr. Thompson, Principal of St. Stephen's United Church College, Edmonton, in 1946 stressed that most of his staff had Ph.D. degrees and were lecturing in the Arts Faculty of the University of Alberta.

Both in numbers and in strength the Bible schools far surpassed the theological seminaries. Between 1922 and 1947 the fundamentalist institutions grew steadily. The total number of students increased from 800 in 1940 to 2,100 in 1947, of whom possibly 200, chiefly at the Prairie Bible Institute, came from the United States. Since over 80 per cent of the male graduates normally applied for ordination, few of the larger sects after 1940 lacked ministers, and, in fact, with the rapid growth of non-sectarian schools like Prairie Bible Institute and Briercrest Bible Institute, some would-be preachers occasionally found it hard to locate an interested congregation.

The theological seminaries, on the other hand, declined in enrolment after 1920, and certain ones even closed down. By 1947, two of the three Anglican seminaries in the West, St. Chad's in Regina and St. John's in Winnipeg, were struggling for life, and the combined enrolment of the three institutions was under 45. The Union Baptists began, as the Minutes of the Western Baptist Conference in 1928 indicate, with a strong belief in the value of a prairie seminary:

The question has been asked as to why Baptists need a training school in Western Canada when they have such institutions as McMaster University and Acadia. Experience of those manning the mission fields in Western Canada leads to the conclusion that the distant training school does not supply the type of personnel best fitted to do the work that is required. The religious problems of the West are different from those of the East, and a Western Institution that adequately meets the situation must be free from restricting traditions and ready and able to meet new and developing situations.

By 1932, the College founded by the Baptists in Brandon had graduated 107 ministers, but soon after it was closed down as a theological seminary. The Presbyterians in 1925 lost Manitoba College in Winnipeg to the United Church. In the three United Church seminaries in the prairies, enrolment dropped from over 100 in 1922 to under 65 in 1946; St. Stephen's at Edmonton had 24 students in 1926, 17 in 1935, and about 12 in 1943. The Greek Orthodox Church during the twenties graduated some 16 priests from a seminary in Winnipeg, but closed it from 1937 until 1946. Only the Lutherans showed any progress in theological education in the West. Two Bible schools were built, one at Outlook, Saskatchewan, by the Norwegian Synod, and the other at Camrose, Alberta, called the Canadian Lutheran Bible Institute, a joint project of the Augustana, Danish, Norwegian, and Lutheran Free Synods. Their combined enrolment by 1946 was about 90 students. Junior colleges offering pre-divinity courses were established by the American, Missouri, and Norwegian Synods at Regina, Edmonton, and Camrose respectively, and theological colleges by the United Evangelical and Norwegian Synods at Saskatoon, but altogether these institutions attracted only a small number of students. The nine non-Roman theological seminaries in the West had a combined enrolment of fewer than 250 students in 1946.

Difficulties faced by the denominational clergy in Alberta stemmed in good part from the fact that the great majority of them were reared outside of prairie rural communities. Before 1914 large numbers of Anglican, Presbyterian, and Methodist clergy were brought over from Great Britain. After the First World War, failing to recruit a prairie-born ministry, these churches and the Baptists began to draw heavily upon eastern seminaries. The situation changed little after 1930. The Anglicans, confronted with very small enrolments in their prairie seminaries, continued to import clergy from the outside with the result that the great majority of their men in Alberta throughout the 1930's and into the 1940's were from England or eastern Canada. After Union, Presbyterian ministers serving in Alberta were almost wholly from the cities of eastern Canada as were the Baptist ministers after the closing of Brandon College. Even the United Church, which had three western seminaries, failed to enlist a strong contingent of prairie-born clergy. The picture differed only slightly in the case of Orthodox, Lutheran, and Moravian clergy. Prairie-born Moravians who decided to enter the ministry had to study their theology in the Moravian seminary in the eastern United States. The Greek Orthodox Church, whose theological college at Winnipeg only began to graduate western-born priests in the mid-thirties, and then in very small numbers, relied largely up until 1946 upon priests imported from Europe. Only certain Lutheran groups, particularly the Augustana, Norwegian,[15] and Missouri Synods succeeded in recruiting a considerable number of prairie-born theological students for service in Alberta, but even they had to bring in many from eastern Canada or the United States. The fact that the great majority of denominational clergy serving in Alberta after 1935 were not native westerners meant they faced real difficulties in becoming acceptable leaders in prairie rural communities. In fact, some of them so rigidly maintained eastern Canadian customs that they became the objects of the western farmers' long-standing irritation with the East.

After the early thirties nearly all the denominations suffered from a continuous shortage of clergy. Church records tell of this shortage

[15]In 1946 almost a third of the Norwegian Lutheran pastors in the West had been born on the Canadian prairies.

and its consequences. The Diocese of Calgary of the Church of England warned of the danger in 1932:

The Church is in danger of losing its hold on the people in many rural districts. The shortage of clergy and the inadequate means of supporting them, the consequent shutting down of certain missions and the attempt to combine certain missions all tend to the weakening of the Church in the country. The Lethbridge Deanery is large . . . yet there are only four ordained men now engaged in the same territory where some years ago nine priests carried on parochial work.[16]

The Bishop of the Diocese had a similar story to tell ten years later:

Very serious shortage of manpower. The number on our active list today is the lowest it has been during my episcopate. On the day of my consecration it was 34. Within a few months it was 40 and for twelve years it never dropped below that figure. Often it was nearer 50 . . . today it is or shortly will be 32.[17]

Among the Baptists, by 1926 there were six Alberta charges without a pastor. In 1936 the Annual Convention lamented "a growing tendency . . . for our isolated brethren who are far removed from Baptist Churches to link up with other denominations where they and their families find religious inspiration and fellowship."[18] During the Second World War the shortage increased, and the Edmonton–Peace River Association reported: "Three more pastors are required urgently to complete our staff in this Association."[19] The Baptist withdrawal from rural areas which resulted from this clergy shortage is summarized in a B.D. thesis by the Rev. L. M. Wenham:

There are sixty-three fewer English speaking Baptist Churches in 1944 than in 1914 . . . i.e. only half as many English speaking rural Baptist churches as thirty years ago. During the past thirty years 21 new rural churches have been added. This means that over eighty . . . have been closed since 1914.[20]

While in 1930 there were 32 Presbyterian clergymen and in 1934 there were 37, by 1938 the number had declined to 28. In that year the Synod of Alberta urged that, in view of the shortage of manpower, the Church appoint "certain men who are well acquainted with the whole work of our Church to appeal to our people for an immediate response."[21] In 1942 there were only 17 ministers. Two years later, the Synod pointed out "that at least nine ordained ministers are

[16]*Minutes of the Synod of Calgary of the Church of England in Canada*, 1932, pp. 11, 13.
[17]*Ibid.*, 1942.
[18]*Minutes of the Union Baptists of Western Canada*, 1936.
[19]*Ibid.*, 1944–5.
[20]"The Baptist Home Mission Problem in Western Canada" (McMaster University, 1947), p. 40.
[21]*Minutes of the Alberta Synod of the Presbyterian Church*, 1938, p. 11.

urgently needed within the Synod of Alberta."[22] The number of Presbyterian clergy in 1946 was 25. Among the Lutherans, the American Synod and the Augustana Synod noted a shortage as early as 1925, and the Danish Evangelical Synod from 1930 on. Other Lutheran Synods, although less seriously affected, acknowledged a lack of men in 1947. Both the Russian Orthodox Church, which had only 12 priests in Alberta in 1941[23] and fewer in 1946, and the Ukrainian Orthodox Church, which in the mid-forties had 7 clergy and claimed to need at least 10 more,[24] lacked men throughout the entire period from 1920 to 1946. In the United Church the number of clergy fell from 294 in 1930 to 226 in 1942.[25] In 1930 the Alberta Conference Report on Recruits for the Ministry noted: "In the Western provinces it is estimated that there should be graduated from each of our four Western Colleges ten men a year to take care of the developments and wastage. At present we graduate about half that number."[26] The Home Mission Committee for 1942 reported: "Our Church is facing a serious situation due to the number of ministers who have entered the chaplaincy and to the shortage of candidates for the ministry. This condition has its greatest effect on the home mission charges."[27]

The reaction of the denominations to lack of personnel was to amalgamate preaching charges. The United Church began to do this as early as 1930. The *Minutes of the Alberta Conference* in 1931 noted: "It is evident that our policy of amalgamating mission fields has been carried to the limit. . . . We deprecate the withdrawal of our Church from many of its frontier appointments."[28] Nevertheless in the next few years amalgamation was speeded up and between 1930 and 1937 some 103 preaching places were abandoned. In 1938 it was reported: "Through a *rearrangement* of work there are nine fewer pastoral charges this year than last. . . . This means fewer preaching places . . . the figures for the year are 788 preaching places, a decrease of 42.[29] The results are recorded in the 1940 *Minutes*:

[22]*Ibid.*, 1944, p. 10.

[23]*1941 Yearbook of the Russian Orthodox Greek Catholic Church of America*, pp. 69, 71.

[24]Interview with Bishop Sawchuk of the Ukrainian Orthodox Church.

[25]J. Hutchinson, "The Rural Church in Alberta" (B. D. thesis, St. Stephen's College, Edmonton, 1943), p. 39. The decline was not limited to Alberta: the United Church had in Canada 696 fewer clergy in 1947 than in 1925. *The General Council Report of the United Church of Canada*, 1948, p. 182.

[26]*Minutes of the Alberta Conference of the United Church of Canada*, 1930.

[27]*Ibid.*, 1942.

[28]*Ibid.*, 1931.

[29]*Ibid.*, 1938.

"Amalgamation of charges . . . has weakened contacts with outlying districts [and] . . . in many cases we are losing ground."[30] In the Peace River area, which had 17 ministers and 6 summer students in the thirties, there were only 12 ministers and 2 students by 1946.[31] As denominational clergy were withdrawn from frontier and rural points, Bible school graduates often moved in and built up new sect congregations.

The extensive education received by the denominational clergy placed them at a disadvantage in competition with the graduates of the Bible schools, the vast majority of whom before 1945 had only a Grade ix education.[32] In the early years only a fraction of the denominational clergy in the West had college training, but in 1925, as we have seen, the United Church made a college degree a prerequisite for theological training and by 1940 the Anglicans, Presbyterians, Baptists, and Lutherans had adopted similar policies.[33] By the mid-forties a large percentage of denominational ministers had acquired a training which made them unable to talk the language of the province's lower classes.[34] Their sermons were laden with theological analysis and the latest findings in sociology, psychiatry,[35] science, or philosophy. The reaction against "intellectual" and modernist clergy was perhaps strongest among Alberta's Union Baptists who more than once refused to accept McMaster graduates assigned to their congregation. For the most part, discontent was passive: dissatisfied parishioners simply left their church and attached themselves to a sect.

The way in which evangelical preachers lived during their Bible school studies prepared them for the strenuous demands and low salaries of prairie rural ministries. The frugalities of Bible school living, with its Spartan-like attitudes to work, study, and meals, the rigorous orientation of students toward a life of missionary self-sacrifice, and grapevine information concerning the meagre stipends

[30]*Ibid.*, 1940.
[31]Article by Rev. C. G. Kitney, *United Church Observer*, July 15, 1947, p. 11.
[32]Graduates from the Nazarene School which required Grade xi for entrance were the only important exception.
[33]Certain Anglican colleges in the West permitted students to take a four-year combined Arts and Theology course leading to the L.Th. degree, and during the war both the United Church and the Baptist Church allowed older students to take a "short course," usually four years in length. In 1946, the Norwegian Lutheran College at Sasakatoon required only a junior college education for entrance.
[34]Cf. L. Pope, *Millhands and Preachers*, (New Haven, Conn., 1942), p. 110.
[35]The writer heard a college-trained preacher in a small prairie village try manfully to reconcile psychiatry and the Christian faith before a congregation of farmers and villagers.

earned by sect preachers all played a part. Salaries were extremely low in the depression. Even by 1942 a "good" stipend for an Alliance preacher was reported to be $720 a year, and in 1946 the average in many sects was only $1,000.[36] Without the training in frugality received at the Bible schools and the emphasis upon the glories of missionary work, some sect preachers would probably have found such conditions intolerable.

On the other hand, the social background of many denominational clergy aroused expectations of income and prestige that tended to disqualify them for effective work among the poorer classes in country and city. Those from middle-class homes had a natural orientation toward goals of comfortable living and social recognition. Years of study at university and theological seminary strengthened expectations of respectable financial and social rewards among students of both working- and middle-class background. Participation in university life generally led to acceptance of middle-class standards of dress and etiquette, recreation and sophistication. Moreover, the exacting financial and psychological deprivations involved in gaining an Arts and Theological education combined with social pressures to adopt a professional attitude toward the ministry tended to reinforce notions of suitable economic and social rewards. The result was that most denominational clergy came to regard the ministry not as a calling but as a profession, the practice of which entitled them to prestige, adequate income, and regular promotions. Such an attitude resulted almost inevitably from the location of theological colleges upon university campuses, the encouragement of a close association of Arts and Theological students, and the comfortable residence and lecture facilities made available to theological students. Behind these influences lay the considerable wealth of the denominations, their stake in secular society, and particularly their acceptance of many middle-class attitudes and evaluations including a high estimation of advanced education. The contrast between the professionalized expectations of the denominational clergy and the attitudes of sectarian Bible school graduates was expressed to the writer by one idealistic United Church clergyman as follows: "Having no interest in a big salary and no degrees, the sects show no emphasis upon professional concerns as in the United Church. In our church one meets all that blessed business of professionalization."

The wives of denominational clergy tended to share their husbands' expectations. As a rule, divinity students married middle-class women,

[36]These salaries were of course often augmented by gifts of foodstuffs.

many of them with college degrees, who rated the success of marriages mainly on financial and/or professional grounds and thus reinforced their husbands' orientations toward respectable churches with good stipends. Women of working-class background often viewed their marriages to ministers as an upward movement in the social scale, and regarded their husbands' careers from a middle-class standpoint. Ministers' wives from England or eastern Canada found it hard to adjust to the socially isolated and vulnerable position they held in small prairie towns, and often influenced their husbands to move either to Alberta cities or back East.[37]

The attitudes of the ministers and their wives played an important part in the excessive turn-over of rural clergy in the denominations and their tendency to return to the East or the United States. The Union Baptists noted as early as 1921:

The problem of pastoral leadership gives us grave concern. To find men who are able and willing to stay with a task long enough to make a definite contribution is difficult. On rural fields the work seems small, results are tardy, members are scattered, removals constant, distances are great and the weather severe, and pastors one after another become discouraged. Our need is men of vision and strength, men who realize the opportunity, men who are not only called to the ministry, but men who are called to the ministry on the prairie.[38]

By the late thirties the turn-over presented an acute problem to most of the denominations; the average rural incumbency had become of less than two years' duration. The fact is that the denominational clergy were educated far beyond the level of their congregations and inevitably became frustrated, intellectually and socially. Small salaries were aggravating not only on financial grounds but because they were disreputable by middle-class standards. They seemed to suggest professional mediocrity and their publication annually in official church year books was damaging to self-respect.

Although church leaders tended to ascribe the high turn-over to low stipends,[39] they recognized to some extent the larger problem. In 1939 the Presbyterian Church in Alberta sent an overture to the General Synod declaring that college training made young ministers unwilling to serve in western Canada.[40] The Report of the Brandon Swan River Baptist Association for 1942 stated: "In the training of the young men we must seek to give them a vision of the fields which

---

[37]Cf. J. Van Vleck, *In Our Changing Churches* (New York, 1937), p. 70.

[38]*Minutes of the Western Conference of the Union Baptists*, 1921.

[39]During the early forties the average stipend in small rural parishes in most denominations was less than $2,200.

[40]*Minutes of the Alberta Synod of the Presbyterian Church*, 1939.

includes more than fine city churches."[41] Rev. J. Hutchinson, in his study of Alberta's United Church rural pastors, noted, concerning the orientation toward urban pulpits: "It is exemplified in the attitude of men who accept a rural ministry as inevitable until they can gain promotion to a city church. It appears again in the widely accepted sentiment which ranks ministers in direct proportion to the population of the town or city in which they serve."[42]

Dissatisfaction with small rural charges, which occasionally led to the inflating of the church membership figures as listed in the denomination's year book,[43] reached its peak during the depression, when salaries were extremely low and chances of moving to "good" parishes remote. According to the principal of a United Church theological college, the rural clergy of that church were seriously disaffected during these years. Enthusiasm for the ministry dropped, some men resigned, and others went into politics. In spite of salary increases in the forties, a high turn-over continued among men serving small rural points. The Bible schools selected and trained young men to minister to farmers and workmen; the theological seminaries trained their students for an urban middle-class ministry. In many respects the rural areas of Alberta constituted for the latter a clergy "farm" in which younger men served an apprenticeship and proved their capacity for a comfortable city appointment.

The grass roots character of Bible schools was nowhere more clearly shown than in the ethnic composition of their student group. Although the student bodies of a few schools were almost one hundred per cent Anglo-Saxon or German-Canadian, in most cases they included a mixture of different ethnic strains. This was particularly true of large Bible schools like Prairie Bible Institute, Briercrest Bible Institute, Calgary Prophetic Bible Institute, Alberta Bible College, Bethel Bible Institute, and the Prairie Apostolic Bible College, each of which had a sizable number of Ukrainians, Scandinavians, and Germans besides students of Anglo-Saxon extraction. New Canadian

[41]*Minutes of the Baptist Union of Western Canada*, 1942.
[42]Hutchinson, "The Rural Church in Alberta," p. 11.
[43]The denominational year book was resorted to by committees appointed to find a new clergyman. A United Church minister said of it: "For whatever you do, you go to the year book. But some of us have learned to take it with a grain of salt. People who want better jobs pad their salary . . . raise the figure in the book . . . whereas the Church Board tries to keep it as low as possible. . . . People looking for a man in the $3,000 bracket, for example, refer to this year book and see who is getting about $3,000. Some men will take an interim $3,000 a year job because it will place them in that category and will improve their chance of a permanent move into that salary class."

students upon graduation often held services in their own language. In 1946, a number of German Baptist and United Evangelical Brethren preachers were still holding services in German, especially in rural areas. It was this kind of bilingual preaching that made possible seventeen German-speaking congregations and an almost equal number of Slavic churches within the Alberta Pentecostal Assemblies of Canada.[44] Preachers in other sects, especially the World Alliance of Missionary and Evangelical Churches, conducted services in the Scandinavian languages; in sects like the Pentecostal Assemblies of Canada, the Church of God (Anderson, Indiana), and the Christian and Missionary Alliance it became the practice to appoint non-Anglo-Saxon ordinands to do special evangelistic work among recent immigrants with a view to organizing congregations. The availability of ministers of non-Anglo-Saxon background enabled numerous sects to serve on a growing scale all the main new Canadian groups. The effectiveness of this activity is indicated by the fact that questionnaires answered in 1946 by United Church and Anglican clergy in Alberta showed fundamentalist groups to be most prominent in villages and towns with a heterogeneous ethnic population.

Unlike the sects, the denominations failed to attract and maintain in Alberta a substantial number of preachers of non-Anglo-Saxon stock. The Church of England in Canada appears never to have given serious thought to the recruitment of priests with bilingual skills or non-British backgrounds. Other denominations, especially the Baptists, Methodists and Presbyterians, tried until 1914 to minister to new Canadians, but with limited success. Baptists concentrated upon Scandinavians and Ukrainians, but as early as 1917 the number of their bilingual preachers, especially among the Scandinavians, dropped heavily.[45] In the early twenties, a short-term Bible school was opened at Wetaskawin by the affiliated Swedish section of the Union Baptists, which quickly enrolled 25 to 30 Scandinavian students. Until 1942, however, the Western Baptist Union neglected to use this school to prepare young men for a preaching ministry. An abortive attempt to standardize its biblical instruction was made in that year, but a few years later the school closed down. By 1946, after over thirty years of work, the Union Baptists had little more than 500 Scandinavian members in Alberta. Their success with Russo-Ukrainians was no greater. In 1942, they had only six Ukrainian workers in the three prairie provinces, a figure which represented little advance over the

[44]*Year Book of the Pentecostal Assemblies of Canada*, 1947.
[45]*Minutes of the Western Conference of Union Baptists*, 1920.

number in service during the First World War.[46] The Presbyterians' mission work with non-Anglo-Saxons consisted in the early years mainly in encouraging the Independent Greek Church (Ukrainian), and training its clergy at their Winnipeg theological college. However, the priests became so Presbyterian in outlook that most of their congregations revolted and the new denomination collapsed. After Union, the Presbyterians organized a small Ukrainian mission, discontinued during the thirties, and several congregations of Hungarians under a single bilingual clergyman. In 1946 this work had fewer than 300 members. The 1944 Calgary Synod of the Church resolved: "Whereas . . . we are failing to reach [many non-Anglo-Saxons] within our bounds, especially the young people, and whereas it is difficult to secure non-Anglo-Saxon workers, therefore be it moved that the Church again set its face to the non-Anglo-Saxon work."[47] To pass such a resolution was simple, to implement it was difficult, inasmuch as this hinged upon the recruitment of bilingual clergy. The United Church in 1926 had three German-speaking congregations and one Ukrainian worker in Alberta. Slight progress was made during the thirties and a few non-Anglo-Saxons took theological training, but by 1940 the missions had declined to their original number.[48] A report presented to the Alberta Conference of this church in 1938 noted:

For thirty-five years Ukrainian work has been carried on under Protestant auspices and no other missionary enterprise among non-Anglo-Saxons in Western Canada augured more hopefully at first, yet none proved so disappointing ultimately. In 1914, there were 33 Ukrainian ministers in Manitoba, Saskatchewan and Alberta, with 117 preaching places and a constituency of 34,000 Greek Orthodox, who were accessible to the missionary. In 1938, there were only eight missionaries in the three provinces. In 1918, in Alberta alone, there were seven ministers and eighteen preaching places. Today there are only three Ukrainian ministers.[49]

Clergy who spoke European languages were difficult to secure and, because they tended to migrate to the United States, where better conditions and salaries were always available, almost impossible to keep. Ultimately, however, the shortage of bilingual clergy was a result of the restricted ethnic and class orientation of church seminaries in both the East and West.

[46]The only non-Anglo-Saxons affiliated in any way with the Union Baptists who showed advance in numbers were the fundamentalist German Baptists.
[47]*Minutes of the Calgary Synod of the Presbyterian Church*, 1944, p. 11.
[48]*Minutes of the Alberta Conference of the United Church*, 1941.
[49]*Ibid.*, 1938. Cf. T. C. Byrne, "The Ukrainian Community in North Central Alberta" (M.A. thesis, University of Alberta, 1937), p. 48, and D. B. Carr, "The History of Religious Education in Alberta" (B.D. thesis, St. Stephen's College, 1942), p. 147.

Bible school students were so selected and trained as to be acceptable to evangelical and puritan groups in Alberta's population. The schools emphasized a fundamentalist outlook, a puritan morality, and an uncomplicated system of sentiments and values. They demanded that applicants for admission be "converted Christians" and adhere to narrow puritan notions of recreation and morality. Thus, the Prairie Bible Institute application form asked prospective students in 1946: "Have you any bad habits, such as smoking, drinking, etc.? Is it your intention to uphold the standards of the Institute with regard to morals, dress and Christian conduct? (Read general information in manual.) Will you abide by the rules and discipline of the Institute and cheerfully obey those over you in the Lord?" Daily Bible study provided numerous arguments against modernism and evolution, and fall and spring revival meetings strengthened evangelical sentiments, aspirations, and beliefs. A Prairie Bible Institute student asserted that such meetings were often effective in restoring backsliders to the correct path. Many schools regulated the hours of rising and retiring, and the length of girls' skirts, forbade the wearing of jewelry, colourful clothes, and cosmetics, and prohibited dancing, smoking, or drinking and even playing checkers and listening to the radio.[50] A programme of athletics and group singing was usually instituted to channel youthful energies into activities considered "safe." Thoroughgoing separation of the sexes was strictly enforced; in some schools like Prairie Bible Institute and Briercrest Bible Institute, men and women had different nights for going down town, for skating on the school rink, and even for promenading on the grounds during the evenings. Through such practices the schools endeavoured to maintain a rigorous puritan and "other-worldly" outlook. Insofar as they succeeded they prepared their graduates for acceptance among people of a strict fundamentalist and puritan point of view.

Church seminaries maintained quite different selection and indoctrination policies. They aimed to turn out polished preachers and enlightened and reflective religious leaders who would be acceptable in the "best" social circles. Because of their modernist, liberal outlook and the acute shortage of recruits for the ministry, most of them imposed few moral, spiritual, or theological requirements to entrance. One prominent United Church clergyman in Calgary admitted: "The

[50]A resident of Three Hills, where Prairie Bible Institute is located, said that his wife could spot P.B.I. girl students not only by their clothes but by their flat, listless voices. He added, "The girls when they first come are often attractive and nice-looking but in two or three weeks after they have been through the mill and have stopped wearing nice dresses and using lipstick, they're all alike."

place where we really fall down is in the selection of candidates for the ministry. Only once have I seen a candidate rejected. The Presbytery Committee does not take their job seriously." As a rule, seminaries assumed, rather than inquired into, the religious beliefs and moral acceptability of applicants. The spirit of biblical criticism and dispassionate ethical inquiry which characterized both Arts and seminary training, especially after 1925, undermined puritan ideas and sometimes weakened basic religious convictions. Evangelicalism, in particular, was often subjected to direct or indirect criticism. The social and intellectual influences encountered at college helped to emancipate theological students from puritan tabus. By the thirties, a considerable number saw no harm in smoking, dancing, card-playing, or moderate drinking. In consequence, many seminary graduates were unable to understand or accept a puritan and fundamentalist ethos, and often found themselves suspect in the eyes of morally and theologically conservative people.

Fundamentalist colleges gave their graduates numerous skills useful in the rural and frontier parts of Alberta. In addition to their training in radio broadcasting, students received lessons in music and usually participated in the school's choir or orchestra. The range of musical instruction provided is indicated in the following excerpt from the calendar of the small Peace River Bible School at Sexsmith, Alberta:

Music: *Music theory.* . . . This course covers the essentials of notation, rhythms, scale building and sight singing.
Ear training. . . . This is a class taken by students who need special attention.
Voice: Training designed to make the student an effective singer of the Gospel.
Conducting: Practical training in song leading.
Piano. . . .
Choir. . . .

Such training equipped students to provide vocal and instrumental solos and to lead singing at church meetings and on radio broadcasts.

Most Bible colleges also gave their students excellent training in public speaking. Courses were not limited to voice production and enunciation, but also embraced techniques of oratory. At the Calgary Prophetic Bible Institute, for example, the public speaking course dealt with all the devices of mass appeal, such as the use of voice, gestures, and timing and the importance of imagery. The result was that Bible school graduates were usually impressive speakers.

The constant round of prayer meetings and revivals at the Bible schools developed in students an aptitude for fervent praying capable of making converts and reviving backsliders. The students were trained to exhibit religious feelings without embarrassment or hesitancy. An account of a "spontaneous" revival meeting at one of the larger

Bible schools illustrates this uninhibited expression of religious sentiments:

When the day began there was nothing to indicate that it was to be an unusual day. The first class was held, then followed chapel when Brother Downey was used of God to bring a special message. This was followed by deep heart-searching. One after another students arose to confess failure, shortcomings and sin. The next class could not be held and indeed throughout the morning the Spirit of God moved upon hearts. There was an unbroken flow of confession and prayer and praise and testimony. The dinner hour was forgotten and the Spirit of God wrought very deeply in hearts. Throughout the afternoon hours the same wonderful working of God was manifest. Many tears were shed, hearts were melted, and broken as the Spirit of God searched us all out. Many were given faith for healing and sought anointing. Everything was quiet, there was no undue excitement, but a deep, definite, powerful moving of the Spirit of God that uncovered things that were not for His glory, and enabled his children to confess and forsake these things. Not until almost 5:30 could the meeting be brought to a close.[51]

Another skill developed at the Bible Schools was chapter and verse memorization of the Bible, a skill which enabled the preacher to arouse a sympathetic response from those in his congregation with a deep respect for the Scriptures. However, some fundamentalists were aware of the dangers of this procedure.[52]

The denominational seminaries not only omitted many of the skills inculcated by the sectarian schools but also developed aptitudes of little use in a rural prairie ministry. Students were instructed in theological and biblical criticism, parish administration, and social and moral understanding rather than in evangelical preaching and techniques of revivalism.[53] The arts of music and radio broadcasting were ignored; a number of clergy working in rural communities privately deplored to the writer their lack of a musical training. Public speaking courses were often given casual treatment. Students rarely secured experience in extemporaneous prayer or revivalist preaching. One Alberta evangelical pastor commented:

The theological colleges are on the spot. They can't give a man the real training for preaching and when the men get out here they don't know how to go about their job and their sermons are dull. And when people can listen and have been used to listening to good men like Charles E. Fuller [a radio evangelist from Los Angeles whose sermons were broadcasted from 400 stations], they are not going to go to church to get a poor sermon.

[51]Western Canadian Bible Institute Messenger (Regina, Sask.), March 1938.
[52]See The King's Herald, year book of the Winnipeg Bible Institute, 1946, p. 43.
[53]A few seminaries had a mild, traditional form of evangelical teaching. An evangelical student movement begun at the United Church Emmanuel College in Toronto about 1940, the Forward Movement, attracted a significant number of theological and pre-theological students between 1942 and 1945. The Varsity Christian Fellowship, another evangelical student movement, was fundamentalist in outlook and secured little support in most seminaries.

Moreover, most seminaries gave little more than nominal attention to spiritual preparation for the active ministry, including the disciplines of prayer and the devotional life. The emphasis was upon doctrine, church history, biblical exegesis, and liturgy, with an occasional concern for the social gospel and psychological validations of Christian beliefs. The training prepared students to interpret the Scriptures, level an exacting ethical critique at modern society, and evaluate fine points of theological doctrine.[54] But it often led to a type of preaching which was too abstract, unconventional, and sophisticated to satisfy the kind of people the graduates were often called upon to serve. Being equipped to deal with the problems and needs of educated, urban, middle-class people, seminary graduates tended to gravitate to the larger towns and cities, abandoning the smaller communities to Bible school graduates.

Specific evangelistic projects involving students of the sectarian Bible colleges also contributed to fundamentalist growth in Alberta. For instance, during the forties, Prairie Bible Institute trained a 30-voice student choir to assist in evangelical rallies in the vicinity of Three Hills. Other schools trained students to take services in nearby rural points. The prospectuses of two urban Bible schools outlined the variety and scope of student missionary work:

Those attending the Institute are given the opportunity to visit hospitals, distribute tracts, conduct street and young people's meetings, visit the sick . . . [do] other practical things.[55]

Every other Friday evening a group of first year students and their Mission teacher conduct a Gospel service in the Jasper Rescue Mission. Other student groups go to the Hope Rescue Mission on certain occasions and there too, bring the message of the Lord. On Friday afternoon several students go to the home of Mr. and Mrs. A. Silke for a children's meeting. These are children from the surrounding districts and about half of them do not attend any Sunday School.[56]

Such projects, carried on by almost all the leading Bible schools, often resulted in conversions. One school reported that its student work won 75 decisions for Christ in a single school year.[57] Another outlined its student evangelistic activities as follows:

A large city offers rare opportunities for this kind of [evangelistic] experience. Almost every known form of Christian service is provided for on our Practical

---

[54]Emmanual College in the early forties began to return to orthodox Protestant doctrine and to criticize liberal theology, but this was not reflected in preaching in Alberta up to 1947.

[55]*Prospectus of the Bethel Bible Institute* (Saskatoon, Sask., n.d.), p. 5.

[56]"Mission Activity of the Christian Training Institute," *1947 Year Book of the Christian Training Institute* (Edmonton, Alberta), p. 12.

[57]*Swedish Evangelical Mission Covenant Yearbook*, 1946, p. 27.

Work roster. Each student receives an assignment suited to his capacity. Statistics do not tell the whole tale, but the following has been accomplished for the Lord. The following figures cover the seven month period ending April 30th last.

Number of professed conversions	254
Number of persons dealt with	2,427
Number of tracts distributed	61,269
Number of sermons preached	171
Number of Sunday School classes taught	692
Number of Child Evangelism classes taught	389
Number of visits made in homes	943
Number of visits made in hospitals	1,556

These figures do not include the large amount of practical work done by the teachers and staff of the Institute.[58]

The Bible school also employed their students for vacation time evangelism. Although some male students went back to farm work during the summer many were available for home mission work and their number was augmented by girl students and members of Bible school staffs. The mid-summer letter of the Alliance Bible School indicates something of the nature and scope of this summer evangelistic work:

As we have already stated, our Dean is off to the West and will be ministering the things of God there. Our Brother Downey has been serving the Lord in Edmonton and Peace River area; Bro. McVety has gone to take his place in Edmonton, and we heard from him today that the blessing of the Lord attended his first service there; Miss Pugh, a teacher and Dean of Women, has also gone to the Peace River area to help in Camp work; Miss Ione Anderson is carrying on S.B.S. work in Red Deer, Alta.; Miss Bassingthwaite has been in Camp work in Alberta. We have three parties of young people in definite ministry; one group of five went east to Manitoba; another group of five went west and will in all probability reach Victoria, B.C., while another trio is making a wide circle of contacts in Saskatchewan and Alberta.[59]

Frequently students stayed in a village or rural area for the entire summer and ultimately succeeded in building up a permanent congregation for their sect. While this summer work strengthened individual sects in outlying rural communities, a large percentage of students in such non-denominational schools as Prairie Bible Institute and Briercrest Bible Institute engaged in similar evangelistic work under the direction and pay of an inter-denominational home mission group called the Canadian Sunday School Mission. The professed purpose of this body was to carry the Gospel to unchurched communities and especially to children and young people neglected in the churches. Under its direction, Bible school students in teams

[58]*The Messenger,* a publication of the Western Canadian Bible Institute, Regina, Sask., May, 1946.

[59]Mid-summer "Letter" of the Canadian Bible Institute, Regina, Sask., July 9, 1947.

of two or three itinerated over a given area, some conducting daily vacation Bible schools and others sponsoring evangelistic missions. These students boarded gratuitously with friends and sympathizers and received the smallest of salaries. Such workers were dispatched every summer into outlying regions of the prairies. By the summer of 1946, 90 of these students laboured in Alberta.

Large-scale missionary or evangelistic rallies held by the Bible schools were another means of aiding the growth of fundamentalism. These two- or three-day rallies, to which friends and relatives of the students were invited, usually attracted hundreds of persons. In 1946, the Prairie Bible Institute's fall conference drew over 2,000. All these people were provided with free board and lodging and spent three days inspecting the institute and listening to special evangelists. Often, backsliders were recovered and the faithful inspired to greater missionary zeal.

The powerful Prairie Bible Institute and the Briercrest Bible Institute merit special mention as agents of fundamentalist growth in Alberta. Their successes in radio broadcasting and grandiose missionary conferences set a pattern for other schools. Their students made up the backbone of the Canadian Sunday School Mission. In addition, the flow of Prairie Bible Institute graduates into sects like the Swedish Evangelical Mission Covenant and the Evangelical Free Church helped materially to advance these groups.[60] Other graduates organized and ministered to a number of congregations of independent evangelical fundamentalists called Three Hill Baptists. After the Second World War, Prairie Bible Institute and Briercrest Bible Institute graduates began almost simultaneously to organize independent Gospel churches which maintained a loose sort of ecclesiastical connection. The Prairie Bible Institute men called their group the Fellowship of Gospel Churches and the Briercrest graduates labelled theirs the Association of Gospel Churches. By 1946, the Association had 13 affiliated congregations in Saskatchewan, while the Fellowship included 6 churches in Alberta. These new groups, in the manner typical of such religious bodies, disclaimed any intention of starting a new sect. Whatever the intention, however, these two bodies soon began to assume the appearance of new sectarian movements. By 1946 the competition between the larger Bible schools on the prairies was becoming so intense as to make the placing of graduates in preaching appointments a problem; the organization of new sects was one apparent solution to this situation.

[60]In the thirties, graduates of Prairie Bible Institute also went into the Christian and Missionary Alliance in Alberta.

The achievements of the fundamentalist seminaries ultimately led the denominations to organize their own Bible schools. The earliest of these were the Lutheran institutions at Outlook, Saskatchewan, and Camrose, Alberta. By 1940, Baptist, Presbyterian, and United Church leaders, asserting that some of their young people had been "lured away" to Bible schools, began to plan schools which embodied the practical training features of the sectarian seminaries but concentrated exclusively upon the training of lay leaders. None of these denominations seriously considered allowing such institutions to usurp the prerogatives of their theological seminaries and prepare men for the ordained ministry. By 1947, only the United Church had succeeded in opening a lay training institute, and it was in British Columbia. The delays involved in establishing this institution, its limited one-year course and strictly lay training function serve to indicate something of the denominations' inability to make either swift or effective adjustment to the need for rural theological seminaries and associated high school departments. This weakness may be laid at the door of rigidities of professionalization and ecclesiastical bureaucracy within the denominations. Thus it was common for resolutions favouring the establishment of Bible schools to be passed by provincial assemblies fairly rapidly, only to be delayed or tabled by the central boards of the denominations. Head office red tape also meant that excellent practical suggestions on Bible school set-up which emerged from direct pastoral experience in Alberta were set aside. The possibility that Bible schools might graduate ordained clergy who would compete with seminary-trained men also slowed down denominational action. The whole apparatus of clerical salaries, prestige, and preferment was threatened by any such development, and so college-trained clergy and seminary teachers stoutly insisted that existing professional standards of theological education be maintained at all costs.[61] In the United Church, even the suggestion that the lay training schools turn out men for the ministerial order of lay preachers was flatly rejected. The result

[61]The development of professionalization was most pronounced in eastern Canada. In the West it was diminished by the realities of a prairie ministry. Thus both the Presbyterian and the United Church Conferences in Alberta were willing in the forties to lower the traditional educational standards required of the clergy. The Presbyterians of Alberta in 1943 accordingly memorialized as follows: "The Synod of Alberta is of the opinion that a too rigid interpretation of the regulations governing the education and reception of men on the part of the Board of Education is one of the prime causes of our shortage of ministers." (*Minutes of the 1943 Synod of the Presbyterian Church of Alberta*, p. 10.)

In 1928 the United Church in Alberta memorialized General Council to waive the requirement of matriculation in theological training. (*Minutes of the 1928 General Council of the United Church of Canada*, p. 185.) Needless to say, these overtures were not acted upon in either case.

was that the denominational "Bible schools" were exclusively devoted to short courses for lay leaders and therefore failed to meet the real challenge of the sectarian institutions.

While the main fundamentalist sects obtained their pastors from the Bible schools, the Jehovah's Witnesses and the Cooneyites secured their leaders through less formal processes. As an integral part of their protest against established churches, a protest which involved a disavowal of a paid ministry and the whole apparatus of professional clericalism, these groups eschewed all theological or biblical training institutions. They also refused to call their leaders by the title of "Reverend." This anti-clericalism appealed to certain types of people, especially to those who had become disillusioned with the worldly behaviour of salaried ministers. In particular, it won a response from persons with strong grievances against clergy disposed to authoritarian practices. In Alberta, this kind of grievance was not uncommon among those members of the Uniat and Russian Orthodox churches who had suffered embittering experiences with an authoritarian priesthood.[62] A few Lutheran clergy in Alberta had also reportedly exercised their authority too zealously and thereby antagonized groups of supporters.

While opposing formal theological institutions, these anti-clerical sects adopted definite procedures for the recruiting and training of leaders. Cooneyite leaders or "evangelists," who itinerated through the rural areas in two's, were recruited from among the more respected and intelligent members of the sect. Men or women who felt "called" to missionary work required only the consent and backing of the provincial "organization" to begin as full-time "evangelists." Having gained such support, they were paired off with an experienced evangelist of the same sex, and gradually mastered the requisite skills through on-the-job experience and the advice of their senior partner. No definite period of time was set down for this apprenticeship or for evangelistic work *per se*. One could theoretically stop at any time. These leaders received donations from friends and well wishers and were supplied with free board and room by fellow-Cooneyites in whose villages they stopped. Their arrival in a town which boasted a Cooneyite group was the occasion for special meetings, at which they delivered the main sermons. Here and at the annual conferences, they were accorded respect and a status similar to that of the apostles

[62]Some observers maintained to the writer that the Russian Orthodox clergy who came to Canada in the first fourteen years of the century were sent there as a punishment for infringements of ecclesiastical discipline in Russia.

in the first century. The heads of the local groups, like the first century "elders" of the Christian Church were only part-time leaders.

Up until 1943, leaders among Jehovah's Witnesses received no formal training. They were of three types: the Service Directors, appointed by headquarters to supervise local branches, the Pioneers, or full-time distributors of literature, and the elected leaders of the local branches, called Company Servants. In 1943, headquarters opened the Watch Tower Bible Society of Gilead in the eastern United States, which gave a five-month training course to leaders selected by the central organization from branches in all parts of the world. Unlike the Bible schools, the Gilead Centre accepted only certified "ministers" who had been Pioneers for at least two years. Pioneers, usually young people, were the backbone of the Witness organization; they went from town to town distributing literature and seeking converts, under the direct orders of the central organization. They received an allowance for room, board and clothing, minimal travelling expenses, and $10.00 a month for extras. Their tasks were often specialized: in the larger cities some were assigned to apartment buildings, others to stores, and still others to business houses; techniques of effective approach were worked out for each type of group approached. In 1943, there were 4,204 Pioneers in the United States and at least 20 in Alberta, most of whom travelled in the area north of Lacombe, and especially in the Peace River district. They penerated into the most remote hamlets. It was for Pioneers that the Gilead School was especially designed.

> Entrance is by questionnaire and invitation through the President's office, . . . no tuition is charged as the Watch Tower Society offers gratuitous education, paying all expenses to and from this institution. In addition, students are provided with food and lodging while attending this course as well as a small expense allowance.[63]

Between 1943 and 1946, 659 persons graduated from Gilead, of whom 350 went into mission fields outside of the United States. In the class of August 27, 1945, there was a small contingent of Canadians. Since Gilead was a post-graduate school, its operation did not alter the practice of securing leaders through the normal activities of the local units. Literature distribution, sandwich board display work, and public speaking practice at meetings provided a great range of activities in which natural leaders could demonstrate their ability and secure recognition.

[63]"The Watch Tower Bible Society of Gilead," *Messenger* (Cleveland, Ohio), Aug. 12, 1946.

The process by which Cooneyite and Jehovah's Witness leaders emerged guaranteed a grass roots type of evangelist. Everyone had to "rise from the ranks." With few exceptions, the leaders were raised in rural communities, shared the educational, economic, and social status of the Alberta lower classes, and were selected indiscriminately from both Anglo-Saxon and non-Anglo-Saxon groups. Their non-professional character contributed to their success among farmers on Alberta's agricultural frontier where there was often a lack of sympathy for salaried clerics. The success of the Witnesses among Ukrainians, also, was related to the fact that the Orthodox church, lacking state support for the clergy in Canada, had to make financial demands upon the laity. This sect's polemic against money-grubbing clergy with whom it alleged "Religion is a Racket," its practice of not taking up collections at services, and its non-salaried ministry appealed strongly to those Ukrainians most irritated by the Orthodox Church's requests for money. The absence of educational barriers to leadership in both the Cooneyites and the Jehovah's Witnesses opened the door for anyone of ability, including New Canadians, placed the emphasis upon qualities of natural leadership, and favoured the rise of strong and determined persons to top positions. Moreover, these sects were relieved of the necessity and expense of erecting educational institutions and becoming tied to established social institutions. The arrangements which enabled Cooneyite evangelists to live off friends and passing acts of hospitality, and Witness Pioneers to support themselves largely by commissions from literature sales, preserved the ideal of a thoroughly sincere and non-professional clergy, largely sidestepped the usual financial problems connected with missionary activities, and facilitated the recruitment of a large evangelizing body that made possible the penetration of remote parts of the province.

The establishment of leadership training institutions by various cult groups was an important factor in the expansion of these movements both generally and in Alberta. The five cults functioning in Alberta in 1946 which operated such institutions were precisely the most successful of the ten cults in the province. These were Christian Science, Unity Truth, Church of Truth, Divine Science, and the Spiritualists. Christian Science operated the Massachusetts Metaphysical College at Boston, Massachusetts, to train "teachers" who in turn instructed would-be practitioners. Unity had a huge school at Kansas City, Missouri; the Church of Truth and Divine Science operated Metaphysical Institutes in West Coast cities and the Spiritualist colleges were largely located in the mid-West. However, the distance which separated these institutions from Alberta militated against their attracting substantial numbers of Albertans or sending many graduates to build up the work in the province.

Like the Bible colleges, the cult schools were on the fringe of the respectable educational system. Spiritualist institutions were usually correspondence schools, open to anyone who paid the fees. The other cult colleges, although less committed to correspondence work, had similarly low admittance standards.[64] The courses seldom exceeded two winter seasons in length, and the curricula included such subjects as healing, spiritual psychology, metaphysical fundamentals, and the Bible. The Unity school specialized in "preparation and presentation of Unity lectures, spiritual healing, human relations and prosperity, and how to apply God to everyday living." After two years of training, graduates from Unity Truth and New Thought institutions were awarded imposing certificates and degrees, such as Ps.D. (Doctor of Psychology), Ms.D. (Doctor of Metaphysics), or D.D. (Doctor of Divinity). Inasmuch as the schools readily conferred degrees, provided popularized instruction on such "interesting" subjects as psychology, and presented practically no academic barriers to the prospective student, their rapid growth after 1930 is not difficult to understand.[65]

Healing cult colleges tended to select a type of leader well adapted to attract and serve congregations whose members were strongly neurotic or neurasthenic in constitution and middle class in orientation. The pastors of the healing groups interviewed by the writer in Calgary all confessed to a considerable history of neurotic symptoms.[66] Each had been forced to meet and deal with grave personal emotional problems over a long period. Also, each admitted to a strong interest in private intellectual study and to a middle-class orientation and set of values. By concentrating upon techniques of mental healing, silent meditation, and private prayer, the analysis of the various emotional

[64]Cf. L. S. Reed, The Healing Cults (Chicago, 1932), p. 81. Even the heads of the colleges did not have to have a university education.

[65]The following comment of L. S. Reed is pertinent in this respect: "Medical sects exist in part because they provide a short cut to those who lack time, money or mental capacity to attain the qualifications demanded of the medical profession. . . . It is not a mere coincidence that the rise of these limited practice groups occurred chiefly subsequent to the elevation and enforcement of high standards for medical practice." Ibid., pp. 110–11.

[66]One leader admitted that he had had seven nervous breakdowns.

"sets" which lie behind different types of illnesses, and methods of effective public speaking,[67] these metaphysical colleges helped the students to deal with their own emotional problems, increased their general self-confidence, and gave them a mission in life. Indeed, participation in the lectures on spiritual psychology, the class work and the enthusiastic group life of the colleges was often in itself quite psychotherapeutic. In consequence, students frequently graduated with a new self-confidence and personal charm, in addition to certain skills in mental healing. While sharing the emotional disturbances and marginal middle-class position of their congregations, they were thus equipped for leadership by techniques and experience which raised them slightly above the level of the group.

The establishment of metaphysical institutes was of considerable importance to the growth of cult congregations for they produced a steady stream of pastors and zealous lay leaders for the local groups. However, the individualistic character of cult doctrine and practice made possible the spread of their ideas by printed literature and the mails and obviated the almost exclusive dependence upon ministerial leadership common to the development of most religious bodies; untrained local leaders could readily be directed from headquarters and supplied with all the requisite literature on the cult's worship and doctrine. Actually, only a few college-trained cult leaders came to Alberta. The work of these few, however, gave a fillip to the growth of Unity Truth, New Thought, and Spiritualism and indirectly aided Christian Science expansion.

[67]Two healing cult leaders in Calgary who had not received formal metaphysical instruction had been trained in dramatics or elocution.

CHAPTER SEVEN

Techniques of Evangelization

IN THE EARLY YEARS of sectarian advance in Alberta dependence was largely placed upon tried and tested evangelistic methods. During the First World War, certain sects began to reach into outlying settlements through an itinerant ministry. One or more travelling evangelists would spend a week in a community, holding a tent meeting every night and two on Sunday. Wherever possible they persuaded interested lay people to open a Sunday school and a weekly cottage meeting. Later the roving district superintendent of the sect would visit or correspond with the leaders, arrange other tent meetings, and, when the congregation was sufficiently strong, send in a regular pastor. The Nazarenes, the Pentecostal Assemblies of Canada, the Apostolic Church of Pentecost, the Foursquare gospel, the Apostolic Mission, and a number of other groups sent out itinerants from the 1920's until 1940, and succeeded thereby in opening up many new congregations in isolated rural areas.[1]

In the early thirties, teams of Bible school students began to travel in rural and frontier districts during the summer, holding ten-day and two-week Bible vacation schools for the children and revival meetings for the adults in the local school building. Sizable numbers of adults often attended the evening meetings, if only out of curiosity and gratitude. By the late thirties many sects were beginning to carry on this kind of ministry to newly settled areas. The Nazarenes, the Disciples of Christ, the Alliance, the Pentecostal Assemblies of Canada, and the Apostolic Church of Pentecost enlisted recruits for this kind of ministry from their prairie Bible schools. With the expansion of the schools, the extent of the work increased. Thus, in 1944 the Alliance sent out forty young men and women, nearly all from their Regina Bible School, to conduct vacation Bible schools in the three prairie

[1]The 1933 report of the Nazarene District Conference of Alberta stated "We have 3 tents that should be busy all through the tent season; 20 new fields should be opened," and listed the towns of Peace River, Crossing, Grimshaw, Calder, New Norway, Bashaw, and Battersea as evangelized by tent meetings.

114   SECT, CULT, AND CHURCH IN ALBERTA

provinces.[2] The Nazarene Church also used trained deaconesses for the work. By 1946, the leading sects were heavily committed to this summer vacation-school evangelism.

Organized in 1928, the Canadian Sunday School Mission[3] was for many years the most prominent fundamentalist institution promoting vacation schools throughout the newly settled areas of the West. In 1939, at its peak, it employed altogether some 300 summer workers in Ontario, Manitoba, Saskatchewan, and Alberta, the great majority being recruited from inter-sectarian Bible schools. Travelling by bicycle, truck, and car, they penetrated into many remote areas. In 1945–6 Alberta's 90 workers travelled a total of 62,000 miles.[4]

The Canadian Sunday School Mission not only ran Bible schools that met in school buildings or granaries, barns, or backyards, but also held evangelistic meetings, organized children's camps, established Sunday schools, published and distributed tracts, and sponsored a weekly radio broadcast from Winnipeg. In 1945–6, 73 Bible schools, 3 children's camps, and 2,108 meetings were held in Alberta.[5] Children in remote districts were also enrolled in Bible correspondence courses. The summer camps and the correspondence courses led to the conversion of many children, who were then instructed to convert their parents. The evening evangelical meetings for the adults were at least superficially effective. In 1945–6, the Mission's statistics for all the western provinces listed a total of 82,000 adults at such meetings and over 900 professed conversions, 506 of them in Alberta. During the period 1928–47, over-all statistics indicate that "9,357 attended summer camps; 66,751 enrolled in summer Bible Schools; 9,297 enrolled in Bible correspondence courses and 725 new Sunday Schools were organized."[6] By 1950, some 29,000 professed conversions had been registered.[7]

An examination of the areas visited by these "Mission" workers in the summer of 1946 is suggestive. It shows they concentrated on the dried-out area north of Hanna, in new settlements around Lloydminster, to the north and northeast of Vegreville, and, to a lesser extent, north of Edmonton. Almost all the places visited were small

[2]*Minutes of Christian Missionary Alliance Conference for Western Canada,* 1944.
[3]The Mission was fundamentalist and Baptist. The total depravity of mankind and the necessity for rebirth were stressed.
[4]*Canadian Sunday School Mission Letter* (Winnipeg), May 1947, p. 8.
[5]*Ibid.*
[6]*Ibid.,* Nov. 1947, p. 6.
[7]*Ibid.,* May 1950, p. 2.

villages. Fifteen of the place names did not even appear on the regulation map issued by the Province of Alberta. Such remote and tiny villages, especially in the north, had been neglected by other religious institutions. The Mission's 1946 prayer letter reported:

Summer Bible Schools have done much to reveal the need of this Northern country. Most of the children had never seen a Bible closely, or heard the Name of Jesus. They had no idea what a Sunday School is. At the end of the Summer Bible School it touched us greatly to see how much they knew of the simple plan of salvation. Twenty-three professed salvation. . . .

Much of the work of the Canadian Sunday School Mission was among non-Anglo-Saxons, especially Germans, Poles, and Ukrainians.[8] Evangelists usually spoke the language of the people among whom they worked and carried literature printed in it. An evangelist stated in the Alberta prayer letter of 1947:

We have two services on Sunday, one in Ukrainian and one in English, and also a Young People's meeting and mid-week Prayer meeting and Bible Study. Then other nights we visit the new converts and have family worship and encourage them to pray and read the Word. Through the day we endeavor to reach the homes of the people who do not attend services. We have some wonderful contacts here. Jack has brushed up on his Polish language as well, and we carry a few Polish hymns with us.

The expansion of the Canadian Sunday School Mission and the building up, during the forties, of a hierarchy of provincial super-intendents with a central director,[9] marked the transition of this movement to the status of a sect. The Mission began to put evangelists in charge of one or more congregations, to conduct services and Sunday schools throughout the year and to supervise the summer students itinerating near their community. By 1946, the Mission had over forty of these permanent evangelists, twelve of whom were located in Alberta; many were young women graduates of the sectarian Bible schools. Summer work became increasingly focused upon districts where support was known to exist. More time was also given to the organization of summer camps and Bible conferences, six of the latter being held in Alberta in 1947. As the administrative

[8]In 1942, the organization reported that 71 Ukrainians had professed conversion. *Ibid.*, May 1943.

[9]"It is not merely the acknowledging of letters and donations, the correcting of Bible Correspondence Courses, the mailing of supplies to workers, and of Bible Memory Contest information and prizes, the preparation of reports, the meeting of many visitors, and other tasks too numerous to mention—not these alone, important as they are. It is rather the binding of all departments of the work into one strong unit. The office, in other words, is the hub of the wheel. . . ." This quotation from the May 1947 prayer letter of the C.S.S.M. attempts to justify the establishment of the provincial offices.

apparatus grew heavier, however, the number of summer workers decreased until there were only only 230 in 1947. The first stage of sect activity, marked by great enthusiasm and rapid expansion, was over. Retrenchment was traceable to difficulties of administration that followed upon early mushroom growth and to competition from Bible schools which employed increasing numbers of students in summer vacation-school evangelism. Also, with institutionalization, the Mission lost its attraction for some of its early workers.

Two sects, the German Baptists and the Cooneyites, engaged in distinctive types of rural itinerant evangelism. The former used unordained full-time evangelists called Colporteurs who travelled extensively and sold fundamentalist tracts from door to door, often penetrating into remote districts. The Cooneyites sent out evangelists "two by two" into countless small hamlets and rural communities. Staying for a week or two in each place, they visited every home in the attempt to organize cottage meetings. Numbers were not important; they were prepared to take great pains to win one convert. Although these two sects seldom won large numbers of converts in any one place, this form of itinerant evangelism did gain new supporters in the more remote and unchurched areas of the province.

The strength of sectarian itinerant evangelism was in its range and flexibility. Because large numbers of students and full-time evangelists were available, fundamentalist groups could cover most of rural Alberta and penetrate into many outlying settlements. House calls reached the lonely and shy, tent meetings appealed to those who liked crowds and music, and literature was provided for the studious. The non-sectarianism of the Canadian Sunday School Mission gave it a special attraction for many. Direct appeals to such groups as young children and isolated non-Anglo-Saxons were also important.

Besides directly strengthening the fundamentalist movement, itinerant "sowing of the seed" opened up to people in remote areas the whole sect "world" of Bible school, fundamentalist radio broadcasting, summer camps, and outstanding city evangelists like Carlson, Lawlor, and Aberhart. When such people had saved some money they often holidayed at a fundamentalist summer camp or went to a Bible school conference. And if they moved to a city they were likely to visit the leading evangelist's church. Itinerant evangelism involved, in short, a widespread advertisement of all the main fundamentalist attractions.

The gradual withdrawal of Alberta's leading denominations from isolated and less populated rural areas of the province, especially after the early thirties, heightened the significance of sectarian itinerant work. Before the First World War the Church of England in Canada had over a dozen itinerant priests in southern Alberta, but by 1922 clergy shortages reduced the number to one,[10] and in the thirties even the one was withdrawn. This meant the abandonment of numerous small rural points, and the limitation of many others to occasional ministrations.[11] Anglican withdrawal in the areas south of Calgary was portrayed in the report of Rural Dean Middleton in 1936:

Before the first war, saddle horses were bought, buggies requisitioned, motorcycles given a trial test, all to "spy out the land" for future developments. Churches were built; mission houses erected, and the whole south was fast under way of being consolidated for the Anglican cause. The "Call to Arms" came in August 1914, when, one by one, these pioneer sons of the Church returned home, leaving behind scattered congregations with few leaders. A doubling of congregations; an extension of districts; an irregular itinerary were all tried with little success, by the few remaining missioners, and in consequence, the self-sacrificing work, so nobly undertaken, became more or less temporarily abandoned. . . . It is not until now, some twenty years later, that the Church has been able to minister once again to all the points instituted in the original area set aside a quarter of a century ago.[12]

The resumption of activity in the mid-thirties was cut short by another shortage of clergy during the Second World War, which curtailed Anglican rural work in all three Alberta dioceses.

The retreat of the Union Baptists from small villages was no less significant. Over 80 of their prairie churches were closed between 1914 and 1944.[13] A shortage of funds and a lack of theological students, especially after 1933, forced a withdrawal of the student summer supply system. From 1936 on, no itinerant evangelists were employed and summer vacation-school work was confined to the cities and larger towns. In the Second World War, the Baptists amalgamated adjacent rural fields and neglected the smaller points.

The Presbyterian Church after 1925, in spite of its fine record in the prewar years, abandoned itinerant work and concentrated largely upon serving the cities and larger towns.

Particularly after 1930, the United Church in Alberta followed a policy of withdrawing from small rural villages and combining adjacent parishes under one minister. Between 1930 and 1945, the number of regular prairie points served declined from 933 to 707.

[10]In the other two Alberta dioceses of Edmonton and Athabasca, the situation was much the same.

[11]"At the present time there are 40 churches where services are being held at long infrequent intervals." Bishop's charge to Synod of Calgary, 1924.

[12]Minutes of 1936 Synod of Calgary, pp. 37–8.

[13]L. M. Wenham, "The Baptist Home Mission Problem in Western Canada" (B.D. thesis, McMaster University, 1947), pp. 40–41.

In the dry region north of Hanna, the number of clergy fell from 53 in 1931 to 31 in 1942;[14] in the expanding Peace River area the number fell from 23 in 1932 to 16 in 1942.[15] Thus, in two areas where the Canadian Sunday School Mission was particularly active, the United Church cut its clergy by about 35 per cent. The number of summer mission students who served outlying rural communities from May to September also dropped, and the promotion of summer vacation Bible schools was limited to the main rural parishes. The need for an itinerant ministry was discussed at United Church Conferences in the mid-forties,[16] but up to 1946 no effective action was taken.

Fundamentalist advance in Alberta owed a tremendous debt to certain evangelists who early recognized the possibilities of radio broadcasting. Indeed, broadcasting was the chief means by which

[14]J. N. Hutchinson, "The Rural Church in Alberta" (B.D. thesis, St. Stephen's College, Edmonton, 1943), p. 56.

[15]Ibid., p. 39.

[16]In 1946 the United Church ministers at Grande Prairie recommended to the Alberta School of Religion a larger parish scheme:
". . . whereby two ordained men, and one or two students, either during the summer, or for a year of practical experience, might work, circuit fashion, a large territory, with one man as senior minister. This senior minister, if possible, should be a man who thinks of rural work as a career, who would stay five or six years at least, on the circuit, have the respect of the people, be thoroughly acquainted with the work, and co-ordinate the coming and going of other helpers who might, as at present, largely be young men, from the East or otherwise, doing a short term of Home Mission Work, after ordination.
". . . Each unit would have a position for one man sufficiently demanding and sufficiently honourable, if you like, to provide a task equal to that of the average town, or small city church minister. . . . Student ministers could be used in such larger fields, rather than being put out on their own to sink or swim. . . . Some young lay preachers, with coaching, might be found in most areas, who would take one service quarter, in such a field, going 'around the circuit.' I see in this an antidote to the 'sects' who gain something we find it difficult to compete with, in that many of their preachers are closer to those who listen to them than it is easy for a theologically trained minister to be always, though he may try. . . .
"Moreover the slogan of 'Visibility and Permanence' . . . tends to be out-grown. It makes for a lack of mobility. The investment of money put into many church buildings would yield more in an investment in 'Cabin-trailer manses.' . . .
"The organization would provide opportunity for experiment with newer methods—use of the radio, correspondence Sunday Schools, co-operation with departments of Extension of Universities, etc., as well as with evangelistic work. Equipment, not possible to provide for the small field, might be bought for a larger unit economically, projectors for movies, etc. . . .
"Moreover similar techniques are employed by such groups as Seventh Day Adventists, Sexsmith, and Three Hills Bible Schools, and others in areas like the Peace River."

the relatively insignificant, unco-ordinated fundamentalist sects of Alberta were welded into an influential and widely recognized movement.

By the end of the twenties, popular interest in radio was high. Because of the prosperous conditions of 1925–9, most homes boasted a radio set. The wheat farmer, deprived of frequent social intercourse by his large acreage, and also the isolated frontier settler and cattle-raiser, found in this new device an antidote to loneliness or scarcity of entertainment, particularly in the long winter months. The novelty of radio entertainment also made it popular in town and city.

The influence of Alberta radio stations was enhanced by the fact that the mountains cut off good reception from British Columbia, and distance precluded listening to eastern broadcasts. Lack of competition from powerful American stations and the absence of natural obstacles to long-range transmission, except for the Rocky Mountains, enabled broadcasts to penetrate into almost all of Alberta and parts of Saskatchewan. Broadcasts from CFCN, Calgary, were even received in several northwestern American states. Alberta's stations thus dominated an enormous and yet homogeneous geographical region, with a distinctive type of social structure. The effectiveness of sectarian evangelistic broadcasts must be considered in relation to this fact.

The first and most successful use of radio for fundamentalist evangelism was made by William Aberhart. In November 1925, only three years after the first radio broadcast in Calgary, he initiated a Sunday afternoon broadcast over station CFCN of his Baptist Bible class then meeting in a Calgary theatre. It was largely through radio listeners' subscriptions that he raised money to build a large church in downtown Calgary. By 1927 he was broadcasting from 3 P.M. to 5 P.M. every Sunday and had opened a radio Sunday school which mailed out Bible lessons weekly to children from 5 to 16 years of age. In two more years his preaching and broadcasting had built up a regular Bible-class following of 700, and won for him over 1,000 rural supporters and a radio Sunday school of over 1,200. During the early thirties he secured more radio time and by 1935 was broadcasting a total of five hours every Sunday. Through his radio work he received invitations to visit and preach at many rural points, and quickly built up congregations at Innisfail and Red Deer. The depression had brought CFCN, then a powerful 10,000-kilowatt station, near to bankruptcy, and Aberhart's broadcasts were one of its biggest sources of revenue. "At this time," the pastor of the Calgary Prophetic Church told the author, "Aberhart could have bought CFCN for $200: it was not clear whether they were supporting us or we were supporting them."[17] In 1935, his radio audience was estimated at 350,000, two-thirds of which was in Alberta.

On Aberhart's entry into politics, the Sunday afternoon broadcast remained the strength of his sect. In 1946, three years after his death, it was still very successful.

After 1932–3, Aberhart's radio evangelism came to exert a tremendous influence in the province. Leaders of his sect asserted that, by the year 1935, his broadcasts had become a provincial institution, as popular as radio and an intrinsic part of it. This was no idle boast but a statement supported by observers of every creed and political persuasion. A typical instance of Aberhart's genius for organization was his provision for different memberships in his radio church, based upon the amount of contribution made. These included a "booster" and an "associate" membership. The actual number of memberships in the different categories was never released to the public, perhaps because it would have partially revealed the income earned by his broadcasts.[18] In consequence, it is impossible to state the exact size of either his radio following or the strength of the Calgary Prophetic Institute for the period of the mid-thirties when the movement reached its maximum expansion. It was recorded, however, that the radio Sunday school had 8,000 children in 1935. Aberhart's emersion in political activity after 1935 prevented him from devoting his enormous energies and organizational talents exclusively to the further expansion of his religious movement. It would probably have eventually become Alberta's largest sect if he had been free to concentrate his time and radio skills on it from 1935 until his death in 1943. In spite of his

[17]A *Calgary Herald* article, June 3, 1939, quoted Pastor Crouse, dismissed by Aberhart from the post of minister of the Calgary church, as saying, "Loans had been made by the Church to a company, to a private individual and one loan of $8,000.00 with interest to CFCN." The money for such loans must have come almost entirely from radio income.

[18]In May 1949 the Calgary leaders of the Prophetic Baptist Church and Bible School, the Revs. Laing and Hutchinson, and their associate leaders withdrew from the Aberhart church, taking with them all the Bible students and 90 per cent of the Sunday congregation, allegedly because Premier Manning and his Board of Management would not give an annual financial accounting of the radio income. The seceding Baptists began a new church and Bible school on the North Hill of Calgary and broadcasted at the former times—1:00 P.M., 3–5 P.M. and 7:30–8:30 P.M. They published an audited account of their income for October 1 to March 31, 1950, which showed a total income of $34,748.99. In the next six months they reported receiving approximately $70,000. A large part of this was earmarked to build a new Bible school, to be called Berean Bible School.

political responsibilities as Premier, he carried on his Sunday broadcasts until his death, and maintained a strong following.

The secret of Aberhart's widespread popularity as a radio orator lay not only in unquestioned rhetorical gifts, but in a special flair for making religious instruction simple and entertaining. He used such devices as mock debates about well-known heretical sects like the Jehovah's Witnesses and the Seventh Day Adventists, the reading and answering of letters from listeners, and dramatic prophecies of political events ostensibly revealed in the Old Testament. This admixture of religion and entertainment enabled him to build up, during years of broadcasting that coincided with the nascent popularity of radio iself, an enormous listening audience composed of people of every religious and social leaning. Listeners included many church clergy and quite a number of Roman Catholic laity. In the main, however, his broadcasts appealed to people who favoured an evangelical presentation of Christianity, and in such a way as to create a new sect and to quicken the entire fundamentalist movement in the West.

In 1927, close upon the heels of Aberhart's entry into radio, the Christian Missionary Alliance bought and began to operate a 250-kilowatt station in Edmonton, called CHMA. The Alliance sold week-day time to other denominations, retaining one hour daily and all day Sunday for its own broadcasts. In 1934, failing to meet new technical requirements imposed by the government, CHMA was sold to the powerful 5,000-kilowatt station CFRN, with the stipulation that the Alliance be allowed to book 6½ hours every Sunday for religious broadcasting. The hours of 11:00–12:15 and 6:00–11:00 P.M. were reserved. The Alliance kept one to two hours for themselves and sold the rest at a small profit to other religious bodies. At first they used their time to transmit recordings of American evangelists and Bible school leaders, but later they produced more of their own programmes, in which sermonettes were combined with fundamentalist hymnody. By 1947, this sect had been broadcasting from Edmonton for twenty consecutive years, the last thirteen on a station with 5,000-kilowatt transmission.

The growth of the Alliance in the period 1930–46 was closely linked to this policy of continuous radio broadcasting. Their greatest concentration of members was in Edmonton and in those rural areas adjacent to it within the reach of station CFRN.[19] The opinion of

[19]More than 70 per cent of their congregations were in this area. The 1941 census indicates that, whereas there were 48 supporters of the Alliance in Calgary, there were 221 in Edmonton.

M. P. Pierson, engineer of station CFRN, was that "90% of the success of the Alliance in Alberta is due to its long, continuous and clever use of radio." A provincial leader at their 1943 Western Conference agreed: "At the height of our broadcasting season, we had over 1500 minutes (20 hours) chucked full of Gospel message. . . . The sum of $200.00 would give every worker in a large city the start on radio that would yield tremendous dividends."[20]

Other sectarian leaders became alert to the success of Aberhart and the Alliance and rushed to get air time. The Pentecostal Assemblies of Canada, the Nazarenes, the Alberta Bible Academy of the Swedish Baptists at Wetaskiwin, and two Lutheran colleges, the Concordia of Edmonton (Missouri Synod) and the Canadian Lutheran Bible Institute of Camrose, bought Alliance radio time on station CFRN. The Seventh Day Adventists and the Jehovah's Witnesses also staged a few broadcasts from Edmonton, including some in the Ukrainian language. In Calgary, the Pentecostal Assemblies of Canada, the Nazarenes, and the Prairie Bible Institute of Three Hills secured air time in the mid-thirties. It is significant that it was these sects and Bible schools which were among the fastest growing religious bodies in the province, and also that the Lutheran Synods which pioneered in radio work were among the few sections of that communion to grow significantly in numbers in Alberta.

Second only to Aberhart's radio work in its immediate impact and subsequent influence was the programme which a Dr. Lowry broadcasted over CFCN in 1938. Lowry, a Moody Institute evangelist, came to Calgary in November of that year completely unknown. Paying double the standard commercial rates for a half-hour period early in the morning, he gave a six-week series of daily broadcasts. In that time he received a staggering total of 5,700 letters, 3,700 of them from Alberta and the rest from Saskatchewan, Manitoba, and British Columbia, most of which enclosed contributions. The greatest concentration of replies came from central Alberta, the farming area settled largely by eastern Canadians of puritan stock.[21] The gross income from the letters was in excess of $10,000.[22] Expenses, including

---

[20]*Minutes of the 1943 Alliance Conference for Western Canada*, p. 29.

[21]Dr. Lowry made a chart on which he plotted the location of all letters received. This chart found its way into the hands of Mr. B. Simpson, evangelist on the Sunrise Gospel Hour, and was inspected by the writer in the latter's office in 1947.

[22]This figure is a conservative estimate, based on the average contribution per letter received in 1946 by Mr. Sawtell, the evangelist in charge of the Heaven and Home Hour. It was said that Dr. Lowry, on returning to California and attempting there a similar kind of broadcast, failed to meet a satisfactory response and lost much of his profit from the Alberta broadcasts.

a suite in the Palliser Hotel, radio time (which cost about $3,000), and the employment of five stenographers left a handsome profit.

Dr. Lowry's programmes were high-powered fundamentalist evangelism. They combined hymns, prayers, and a heart-stirring evangelical message which included frequent references to sexual problems. His talks were reported to have made at least 1,000 converts in Alberta. Miss E. Dobbs, provincial organizer for the Varsity Christian Fellowship, whose work took her into every part of the province, stated in 1946: "One still finds numerous converts of Dr. Lowry's all over the Province. They have not backslid, but have remained faithful, and now occupy important positions in various churches." Other evangelical leaders were similarly impressed by Dr. Lowry's achievements. Pierson, the CFRN engineer, asserted that "Dr. Lowry put daily radio broadcasting on the map in Alberta."

Lowry's success led to the inauguration of two influential week-day religious broadcasts, the Sunrise Gospel Hour and the Heaven and Home Programme. After Lowry returned to California he told a young "independent" Baptist preacher named Sawtell of the amazing radio opportunities in Alberta. Sawtell came to Calgary in 1939 and with a pianist named Kelford began a Sunrise Gospel Hour on station CFCN. Later Sawtell sold his interests and began a daily half-hour programme called the Heaven and Home Hour at 8:00 A.M. on CFRN, Edmonton. This broadcast soon won a wide following, estimated in 1946 by the station manager as between 80,000 and 100,000. Sawtell organized his programme on a business-like basis, incorporated it in 1942 with a seven-man Board of Governors, and instituted a semi-annual audit. By 1945 the staff included five full-time and two part-time assistants. By this time contributors to the programme were receiving an annual statement of their donations for income tax purposes. The books of the organization for 1945 and 1946 revealed a steady increase in gross income from $2,500 a month in June 1945 to $5,000 a month in July of 1946.[23] During the winter, the best season for evangelistic broadcasting, letters poured in at the rate of almost a hundred a day. In 1946, Sawtell extended the coverage of his programme, rebroadcasting it at 1:30 P.M. from station CFRN Edmonton and transmitting it by telephone over CFAC Calgary at 3:00 P.M. Thus the Heaven and Home Hour was on the air three half-hours every week-day on two 5,000-kilowatt stations, which together almost blanketed the province. The programme had become an influential force in the fundamentalist movement; it was also big business.

[23]Mr. Sawtell kindly permitted the writer to inspect the books of his company.

The financial success of Sawtell's broadcast in 1945 and 1946 was partly the result of novel techniques for persuading listeners to continue writing letters and forwarding contributions. Such schemes were required because the government now prohibited the direct soliciting of money on the air. Sawtell offered his listeners religious books, pictures, or other articles at attractive prices. Rather than forwarding only the requisite 75c or $1.00, most listeners enclosed $2.00 or $3.00, thus providing the programme with a handsome profit. The evangelist also inaugurated the "Fifty Club Plan," whereby "fifty people pledging themselves to give twenty-five cents (25c) a week toward the support of a missionary, the Heaven and Home Hour will become responsible before God to maintain that worker personally on the field. In some cases the cost is more than that supplied by the Fifty Club, but this amount acts on an average; the Heaven and Home Hour cares for any difference."[24] Contributions went to support foreign missionaries employed by American fundamentalist missionary societies such as the China Inland Mission, the missionaries usually being graduates of Bible schools not attached to any sect. To provide personal contact between contributors and "their" missionary, "Each Fifty Club member is supplied with the name and address of the missionary supported, and, when such is possible, a lovely photograph."[25] By the summer of 1947, the scheme was financing twenty-five missionaries, an achievement which greatly enhanced the prestige and appeal of Sawtell's work. This device gave Sawtell a means of counteracting charges of racketeering as well as augmenting his income, since contributors usually sent him a donation along with their gift to the Fifty Plan.

The other daily broadcast to emerge from Dr. Lowry's campaign eventually outstripped Sawtell's. Shortly after Sawtell's partnership with Kelford broke up in 1941, a young American Bible school graduate and ex-orchestra leader, Rev. J. D. Carlson, at that time pastor of the Edmonton Alliance Church, bought out Kelford's interests, including a religious book store in Calgary, and took over the Sunrise Gospel Hour. He broadcasted over station CFCN, Calgary, from 7:15–7:45 A.M. and 10:15–10:30 A.M. every week-day. Carlson, a natural stage and radio personality with exceptional musical

[24]Pamphlet outlining the Fifty Club Plan. The estimated annual cost of supporting foreign missionaries in the main American fundamentalist societies was $600 a year. This plan was reminiscent of a scheme of Aberhart who in 1927 exhorted his radio audience to contribute 25c bricks towards the building of his Calgary church.
[25]Ibid.

talent, developed a lively and entertaining programme which embodied the same elements as Sawtell's but was more informal. He also sold cheap religious books and made appeals for foreign missions. By 1946, according to his own estimate, probably slightly exaggerated, his radio audience totalled about 500,000. He received over a hundred letters a day in the summer and 300 to 400 during the winter.[26] In the spring of 1947, Carlson left Edmonton,[27] selling his interest in the Sunrise Gospel Hour to the Rev. B. Simpson, a graduate of the Prairie Bible Institute who had been a foreign missionary. As part of the "business," Simpson received a mailing list of 8,000 contributors. The latter did not anticipate the great success which Carlson had enjoyed, and was not disappointed that his daily mail-bag in July of 1947 only amounted to from 70 to 90 letters.[28] This flow of mail indicated, however, that daily evangelistic broadcasting was not entirely dependent upon individual radio personalities.

Alberta's two major daily broadcasts won support predominantly from rural and frontier districts. "Our response is from the unchurched districts and from the small towns and farming areas," Carlson told the writer. Sawtell stated: "Every day people write in and say they are twenty-five miles from the nearest church and enjoy our programme so much." Both programmes were especially popular in the Peace River area. In the years 1944 to 1946 the radio evangelists were beseiged by requests to take Sunday services or preach at midweek evening rallies in rural areas. One leading Edmonton sectarian observed:

Carlson has had considerable influence out in the country through his radio work. He reached out over a wide area, and being a popular personality had a considerable personal following. When people wanted someone to pep up work in a town, or try to get folk together for a new work, they would contact Carlson and bring him in.

Carlson himself said:

The United Church are having trouble getting ministers and have left some towns without regular supply. For instance, at Barrhead, some 70 miles north of Edmonton, they only held services once every three weeks. And yet it was a

---

[26]This figure probably represents the intake in the best two or three winter months. Three stenographers were employed full time at the Alliance Church to take care of this mail.

[27]Carlson then began his own evangelistic mission in the United States, called the Gospel Lifeline Home and Foreign Mission Society, but later, in 1949, went to the largest Alliance Church in Toronto, the Avenue Road Church, earlier made famous by the Rev. "Chuck" Templeton.

[28]Owing to farming activities, July is one of the slowest months in the year. The response in the winter is usually at least 100 letters better than in July.

town of 600 people. I held a service there on invitation and the community hall was crowded out. After the service we organized a branch of the Christian and Missionary Alliance.[29]

Daily evangelistic broadcasts were well received in rural and isolated districts because they were adapted to the needs of the community. By using a time early in the morning, 7:15 to 8:00 A.M., the broadcasts coincided approximately with the breakfast hour or early slack period among farmers and working-class people in town and city. Carlson's second broadcast at 1:15 P.M. and Sawtell's 3:00 P.M. programme, also, were timed to meet a slack period in the routine of housewives. Carlson by using the 10,000-kilowatt station CFCN, and Sawtell by using CFRN and CFAC, were able to reach into almost all parts of Alberta, as well as large sections of Saskatchewan, Manitoba, British Columbia, and the northern United States. Few were the isolated rural areas in Alberta that were out of reach of these programmes. Moreover, in many communities, the listener had practically no choice of programme; at 7:00 it was Carlson or nothing! The programmes themselves, with their stress upon familiar evangelical hymns, short practical prayers, lively musical numbers, breezy informal announcements, and a short talk on the Bible or some simple Christian teaching, were calculated to meet important social needs, especially among rural and isolated people. They relieved boredom, aroused pleasant memories of religious hymnody, provided a personal association with a lively, enthusiastic personality, and furnished moral inspiration and religious comfort. Particularly during the Second World War when life was so often touched by the tragic, and radio stations persistently blared out their chilling war news, evangelical messages of comfort and hope met a widespread need for dogmatic reassurance. Perhaps the success of the two broadcasts can be largely attributed to their mixture of simple religious inspiration and sheer entertainment. Mr. McGuire, manager of CFCN, and a serious critic of radio preachers, emphasized the second factor as follows: "In radio you need showmanship. To be a success you've got to entertain the public; these two men do."

Over the years 1941–6 the influence of these broadcasts upon Alberta's religious development was quite significant. They drew hundreds of isolated evangelicals into some kind of organized relationship with the fundamentalist movement. They led to the establishment of a number of new sect congregations, especially for the Christian

[29]Only a few of Carlson's rallies concluded by the organization of a branch of the Christian and Missionary Alliance.

and Missionary Alliance. Many individuals were drawn away from the denominations. More important, perhaps, these broadcasts maintained and strengthened unnumbered thousands of Albertans in fundamentalist and evangelical beliefs and practices, especially people cut off by distance, infirmities, or other impediments from active participation in a sectarian congregation. At the same time, their campaigns on behalf of foreign missions not only provided openings for Bible school graduates in the foreign field, but, through constant references to specific schools and praise for their work, contributed to the student enrolment and financial position of these institutions.

By the mid-forties the dominance of Alberta's airwaves by fundamentalist evangelists and preachers had become a phenomenon of striking interest. In Calgary, in 1947, fundamentalist sects were on the air 7¾ hours on Sunday as against 5¾ hours for the institutional churches. In Edmonton, also, fundamentalists predominated in Sunday broadcast time, the ratio in 1946 being 6½ to 4 hours. In Grande Prairie, up until 1945, evangelicals had a similar edge over the churches. During the week the situation with respect to the churches was even more unfavourable. The free-lance programmes of Carlson, Sawtell, and an independent evangelist named Jewel, and the 15-minute daily broadcast over CJCJ, Calgary, of the Nazarene pastor, Rev. E. Lawlor,[30] gave to the fundamentalist viewpoint an uncontested air monopoly from Monday to Saturday.

The only place where fundamentalist dominance of the radio was challenged up to 1946 was in the Peace River district. For some years, religious broadcasting on station CFGP, which was opened in 1937, had been largely monopolized by sectarian leaders including Fuller[31] of California, Principal Maxwell of Prairie Bible Institute, and the leaders of the Grande Prairie Bible Institute.[32] In 1944, the Swedish Evangelical Mission Covenant of Canada, under the direction of the Rev. D. Fudland, sponsored two daily broadcasts of 15 to 30 minutes' duration respectively. The morning broadcast consisted of evangelical hymns, while the afternoon half-hour included hymns,

[30]This station had only a coverage of up to 100 miles from Calgary and so Lawlor's programme was not widely heard.

[31]Fuller is a high-powered California evangelist whose daily transcribed programme was broadcast all over the United States and to parts of Canada.

[32]"Radio religion was a bonanza in Peace River for a few years. Radio evangelists have received contributions ranging from four to six thousand dollars for campaigns varying from a few weeks to over a year's duration. But for five of these nine years, no regular voice from one of the older churches was heard on Sunday over the air." From an article by Rev. C. G. Kitney, Grande Prairie, *United Church Observer*, July 18, 1946.

musical numbers, and a religious talk. The story of the immediate success of this enterprise is given in the 1944 *Swedish Evangelical Mission Covenant Yearbook*:

Already by the second month, we were receiving more correspondence mail than any other program, either religious or secular on the station. . . . We pay commercial rates for the afternoon period while the forenoons are on a sustainer basis. Besides the broadcasts we go out to various places for special evangelical efforts. These have been very well attended with often several hundred people gathered and at most of these places there have been souls saved.[33]

Curiously enough, in spite of its proven interest to the isolated rural communities of the area, the broadcast was terminated abruptly in 1945. In the same year the churches finally became active and the Grande Prairie Ministerial Association organized a 15-minute daily devotional programme in which clergy of the regular Protestant denominations and a few of the more respectable sects participated on a rotating basis. The programme soon won considerable support. This venture in broadcasting witnessed to a nascent interest in radio work among the younger church clergy who were at this time stronger proportionately in the Peace River area than in many other rural districts of Alberta.

Radio broadcasting strengthened the fundamentalist movement at crucial points: it added substantially to the membership of certain sects, particularly the Calgary Prophetic Baptists, the Alliance, the Nazarenes, and the Pentecostal Assemblies of Canada; assisted the expansion of prominent Bible schools; upheld evangelical influence in remote areas formerly only accessible to itinerant evangelists; and promoted co-operation among the more powerful evangelical groups. The intense competition for listeners among the daily broadcasters placed individual radio evangelists on their mettle and resulted in devices for widening popular appeal. Evangelistic radio superiority during wartime prosperity meant that the sects acquired funds which hastened the enlargement of five Bible schools and the extension of radio facilities.[34]

Fundamentalist broadcasting succeeded because it was suited to the medium and to Alberta's predominantly rural population. Radio required that programmes be simple and entertaining, and, to a large extent, focused upon one strong personality; it favoured programmes giving pat answers and expressing stereotyped opinions.

[33]*Swedish Evangelical Mission Covenant Yearbook*, 1944, p. 21.

[34]During 1946 the following schools were adding extensions: Alberta Bible College, Alberta Bible Institute, Prairie Bible Institute, Canadian Nazarene College, and the Christian Training Institute.

Sect programmes met all these requirements inasmuch as they were simple, naturally folksy, lively, and usually built around one personality. In fact, radio provided precisely the kind of rostrum that most appealed to fundamentalist leaders for it gave them vast scope for publicity and exhibitionism. McGuire of CFCN declared: "Some men [among the evangelists] get microphonitis—they need publicity. Indeed, they die a slow death if taken off the air." Such sect broadcasters as Aberhart, Lowry, Sawtell, and Carlson received something of the sort of devotion generally accorded outstanding radio crooners and comedians. The scattered nature of rural settlement in Alberta and the existence of numerous isolated "frontier" communities accentuated the importance of entertaining broadcasts and popular radio personalities. The simple, informal, homespun manner of evangelical broadcasters, their showmanship, and their use of popular hymns increased their appeal to the farmers and urban lower-class groups. Radio broadcasts also provided a cheap form of advertisement for urban sects. Rev. E. Lawlor of the Calgary Nazarene Church stated, "My radio broadcasts help me a lot—bring in a lot of contacts. My bill for advertising in any former church was very high but I get along here on very little, because radio does the job." Urban radio preachers found that their broadcasting aroused interest among rootless city dwellers and attracted farmers and small townspeople who, on moving to the city, wanted to see the people whom they had heard on the air.

The centralized form of administration common to the denominations delayed their entry into radio, even when this was urged by local clergy in Alberta. For instance, in the late twenties Rev. Rex Brown of the United Church in Calgary recommended to the Home Mission Department of his church that they establish week-day broadcasting; his recommendation was ignored. During the thirties, the Alberta assemblies of the Anglican, Baptist, Presbyterian, and United Churches all discussed religious broadcasting, but no concrete action was taken. In the early forties the Anglican, Baptist, and United Churches set up radio committees which brought in comprehensive reports and recommendations. But since proposals had to be funnelled through central boards, time was lost and resolutions drastically modified in their sweep and effectiveness. An indication of the interest in radio evangelism in the forties and the difficulty of securing appropriate action is evident from the minutes of Alberta conferences of leading denominations. The report on radio of the 1946 Synod of the Anglican Diocese of Athabaska in northern Alberta stated: "A petition was prepared and passed humbly calling upon the General Synod to set up a Commission on Broadcasting which would be associated with the Committee on Evangelism." The minutes of the Conference of Western Baptists in 1944–5 reported:

An appeal was made to all churches to find out if and when they used radio for broadcasting. Only one reply came to this request. They pointed out that there are 31 radio stations in the West, Manitoba 4, Alberta 8, British Columbia 12. Other denominations are setting aside large sums of money for the radio work, but Baptists in the Dominion are doing very little if anything in this direction.

In 1945 the Committee of the Presbyterian Church on the Needs of the West reported a pressing need for "the reaching of our people by the use of literature and radio." The extent to which use was made of radio by the Presbyterian Church in Alberta at that time is illustrated by the following item: "Rev. J. B. Miller in the North and Rev. E. G. Garvin in the South broadcast regular morning services once a month in order to reach those who have no contact with the church." The minutes of the 1943 Conference of the United Church in Alberta contained many references urging radio evangelism:

[The Radio Committee] was appointed as a result of a meeting of the Conference Executive, which felt that no time should be lost in formulating a radio policy for the Alberta Conference. . . . Our men are very much concerned and are giving the subject serious thought.

While our Church is represented very ably on the Religious Advisory Council there is no Committee of the United Church of Canada on Radio. . . . We therefore recommend . . . that a Radio Committee for the whole Church be set up, whose duty would be to supervise and co-ordinate all United Church broadcasting throughout the Country, and to work with Radio Committees of the various Conferences. . . .

We took cognizance of the gains registered by the "Sects" in recent years, due to a large exent to an extensive use of the radio. . . . In our opinion programs originating in Toronto do not serve the needs of our people as would broadcasts originating in Calgary, Edmonton, Grande Prairie and Lethbridge. There must be a strong element of Community interest. . . . We think that a Religious Forum of the Air, in which religious, moral and personal problems are discussed, alternating with a warm evangelistic message, delivered from our point of view, and with a systematic presentation of the doctrines and teachings of our church, all of course dressed up with appealing music, would be most effective. . . .

We believe that the time has come when the United Church, by way of experiment, should set apart a few men for a distinctive Radio Ministry. . . . With the scarcity of Ministers and the closing up of many country appointments this might be a most effective type of Home Mission Work.

The minutes of the Alberta Conference the next year, however, indicated that no progress had been made:

Last year we recommended that the Conference undertake half-hourly weekly broadcasts from Grande Prairie, Edmonton, Calgary, Lethbridge.

This recommendation was not implemented (1) because your Committee considered it wise to wait and see what the Church's Commission on Radio might be prepared to do, and (2) because enquiry made it clear that a Conference programme released through an Alberta network is impracticable, and that even local programmes, arranged, financed and supervised by a Conference Committee presented very serious difficulties. Your Committee now feels that if anything is to be done over local stations it will have to be initiated by local committees. . . .

Finally, in 1946, the committee secured grants of $1,200 for Grande Prairie and $750 for St. Stephen's College, Edmonton. However, the recommendation that a full-time radio evangelist be secured for Alberta was tabled, in spite of the fact that the church had just such a man at Prince Albert, Saskatchewan.[35] Anyway, by then, it

[35]A letter written on July 25, 1946, by the Prince Albert radio minister to the United Church clergyman at Grande Prairie gives insight into the problems of daily religious broadcasting faced by denominational clergy:

"Our station has a large coverage of the Northland. It is a five thousand watt station. . . . The trouble with contacts on the field is this: so many of our Church people are isolated in little pockets among other groups, such as Roman Catholic and the like, that we can't get in to them. We meet them when they come to the hospital or Sanitarium. . . . It is these people that we are chiefly concerned with. The radio is the only means of service that they have.

"Every morning we have fifteen minutes free time for morning meditation. This alternates between the churches. . . . The station also gave us free time for our "All Aboard for Adventure Series." The response to this was most encouraging. Then we have two other periods that we have to pay for, one half hour on Thursday (Counsellor) and one half hour on Sunday night. . . .

"The work of the Counsellor is . . . along the lines of pastoral psychiatry. One broadcast might deal with tensions, nervous breakdowns. After such a broadcast I had a letter from a Doctor who wanted to know how to get the peace I had spoken of on the air. He had had a nervous breakdown. I was forced through these letters to do some digging. I took a ten-lesson course on psychosomatic medicine—along the line of Glenn Clarke's Camps Farthest Out. One has to be careful, of course, along lines like these.

"The matter of full time radio work is something that I am wondering about myself. I am of course on full time. First of all my handicap in full time is finances for expenses. . . . I use a great deal of musical background on broadcasts. I do it purposely to capture a certain type of listener. I find that fifteen minutes' speaking is the outside limit of holding the average listener. You are good to do that. You must be absurdly simple. You cannot be simple enough. . . . Then I would like to be able to follow up with books and booklets if I had the money. Travel expenses are my 'bug bear.' The old car drinks the gas on some of the roads I travel. . . . There is no doubt that radio is a full time job. I have been doing my own typing, writing, and what have you, and it takes hours of time. There are letters I have to spend time on. . . . If I could talk to people it would be much more satisfactory, but I doubt if they would talk face to face. . . . Radio full time is great work, but it is also heartbreaking work. You have your Committees, your church to sell on it; even yet they watch to see if you leave the beaten orthodox way of doing things on the Air. . . .

"We have received this year from individuals about five hundred dollars and from Churches, Ladies Aids, and W.M.S., etc., about six hundred and fifty. . . . This is still short of the required amount for the broadcasting year. . . . We need not expect to have great returns for some years to come. I suppose we could

was too late to break into radio broadcasting in a big way. By the early forties nearly all the time available for religious broadcasts was under contract. The Radio Committee of the Alberta Conference of the United Church reported in 1944:

> We call attention to the difficulty of initiating local programmes owing to the fact that on many stations there is no time available. In certain instances the smaller sects have cornered all the time which the stations feel they can devote to religious broadcasting, and the United Church, whose people constitute a large percentage of the listening audience, is without facilities for reaching its people.

McGuire of CFCN, Calgary, explained in 1946:

> We're always under pressure from the religious groups for more time. But we must be loyal to our old customers. . . . When we tell ministers that Sunday is crowded out, they ask for a week day hour. But a quarter hour of religious program would require the right kind of programs both before and after, in order to protect our listeners. That would mean three-quarters of an hour of religious or semi-religious broadcasting—for only $15.00. We just can't afford to do that!

Another factor militating against the churches, according to McGuire, was that "too many of the ministers don't know how to put over a good broadcast. Many ministers don't realize that radio is entertainment . . . they want to talk all the time." The churches' failure to train their seminarians in radio techniques meant that their broadcasts were often wooden and unimaginative, and in language, musical numbers, and general tone largely of middle-class appeal. Moreover, by broadcasting over stations with a restricted range, they failed to tap the great mass of rural listeners.[36] In consequence, denominational programmes did not draw a sufficient response to pay broadcast costs.

The denominations failed to master the radio technique because swift and effective action was inhibited by tendencies toward conformity, respectability, careerism, and centralization of policy. Action was delayed until centralized or inter-denominational schemes, functional to denominational goals and the system of a professionalized clergy, were finally organized. Meantime sectarian broadcasters had seized the best allotments of air time and gained a wide and steady

---

if we used high pressure salesmanship. I detest it, and don't hope to do it. In fact it is breaking the CBC regulations to go outside their prescribed form to appeal for funds. But some of the groups do it and seem to get away with it."

    This letter is reproduced in part, owing to the kindness of Rev. C. G. Kitney.

    [36]Sect leaders knew that to get funds for broadcasting they had to reach the rural masses. Rev. H. Paul of the Pentecostal Holiness Church, Calgary, observed: "Indirectly my broadcasts more than paid for themselves, for they brought in members. However, since they were only on CJCJ (1000 kilowatt) they did not bring in a high return; the money is out among the country people."

listening audience. It is significant, too, that their kind of evangelical programming was similar in character to successful secular broadcasts such as soap opera drama, mystery stories, cowboy and jazz music. Thus, sectarian broadcasts were able to consolidate the alignment of the fundamentalist movement with broad lower-class groups in city and country, whereas formal, dignified denominational programmes appealed mainly to the small middle class.

The cults did not use the radio extensively in Alberta, although they were not insensitive to its possibilities. Unity Truth claimed to be the first organization in the United States to give religious broadcasts, and by 1939 eleven stations in the United States carried Unity programmes regularly.[37] However, few of these broadcasts reached Alberta and the local Unity group showed no interest in radio work. Christian Science broadcasted from Calgary a few times during the early forties, and Miss Chew broadcasted weekly in the same period, first as leader of the Church of Truth and later as minister of the Divine Science church. Her Divine Science programme, entitled the "Art of Living," was carried at 10:00 A.M. on Sunday mornings on CJCJ. Miss Chew had a quiet, refined manner, a good radio voice, and a fine command of English. The fact that her programme was carried on a 1,000-kilowatt station was no special handicap, inasmuch as her lectures were addressed to urban, educated middle-class people, not to rural listeners. By 1946 her broadcasts had begun to win a hearing. The 1947 Church of Truth leader, Rev. E. Cooperus, said that he was convinced Miss Chew's broadcasts had added members to her group and that he planned to get radio time himself as soon as possible. In general, however, lacking an orientation toward the farming population, the cults made little use of radio.

Sectarian groups in Alberta consistently employed newspaper advertising for promotion and evangelism. Fundamentalist advertising in the Saturday edition of city newspapers was in certain years extremely lavish and colourful. Examination of the *Calgary Herald* revealed that the years 1917, 1920–21, 1931–3, and 1941–6 were times of extraordinary sectarian advertising. The more colourful advertisements emphasized either a new prophecy or some such attraction as a world-famous evangelist, a unique gospel singer, or an instrumentalist. Some advertising captions that appeared in the *Calgary Herald* are:

Prophecies in the book of Samuel!
Evangelist F. W. Johnson will speak on "The Great Red Dragon (Revelations) What does it symbolize?"

[37]*Unity's Fifty Golden Years* (Kansas City, Mo., 1939), pp. 91–2.

The Rev. A. Cuthbert will give a series of lectures on "Cataclysmic Change and the American Continent—New World, New Age and New Dispensation."
Is the World Ripening for Judgment?
Amazing Boy Wonder [Jack Barry] to lecture Sunday.
Topic: How to be a Success in Life and Avoid Bad Luck. Hear these soul stirring dynamic lectures that stirred two nations.
Revival Meetings with the Musical Carletons.[38]

In later years advertisements tended to become smaller and to use less melodramatic, more stereotyped phraseology. Thus, Aberhart's conspicuous 6″ x 6″ ads of 1923 which began "R U 2 Ready . . . " had become much smaller and more dignified by 1940. Nevertheless, up to 1946, evangelical newspaper advertisements in Calgary and Edmonton were clearly distinguishable from the small,[39] formal notices employed by the churches. The former were designed to catch the eye and awaken interest; the latter were little more than announcements of time of service and sermon topic.

In both Calgary and Edmonton, the evangelists with growing congregations were those who employed large and colourful advertisements. Thus the ministers of the Nazarenes, the Pentecostal Assemblies of Canada, and the Alliance testified to the writer concerning the value of their newspaper displays. On the other hand, sects with stationary congregations such as the Holiness Movement, the Standard Church of America, the Free Methodists, the Swedish Evangelical Mission Covenant, and the Regular Baptists used small stereotyped advertisements. Not only did sensational publicity attract larger congregations but the nature of a sect's advertising often indicated whether it was flourishing or stagnant.

The aim of newspaper advertising was to reach the floating population. The continual rural-urban drift and conditions of social and economic instability brought a sizable number of people to the cities, especially during the depression and the two world wars. Calgary and Edmonton's role as "loading" points for new economic enterprises and as centres for extensive rural hinterlands accentuated the rootlessness of their populations. Among the footloose and mobile were a number of evangelistically inclined people, many of them uneducated and unsophisticated, who were susceptible to striking fundamentalist appeals. Thus Mr. H. Fraser, a leading layman of the Calgary Pentecostal Assemblies of Canada and a business man who knew the Alberta situation intimately, declared to the writer: "I believe there

[38]*Calgary Herald*, Jan. 24, 1917; Feb. 7, 1920; Feb. 1, 1936; July 27, 1946; Jan. 4, 1936; July 27, 1946.
[39]The larger churches of the denominations displayed fair-sized ads during the war years.

are more religious floaters in Calgary than any other city I have ever seen." Edmonton also had a large number.[40] It was to this uncritical, unstable element which was "ready to pack the place that promised the most"[41] in evangelical enthusiasm and novelty that fundamentalist advertising was mainly pointed. Sect leaders were highly sensitive to the existence of this floating evangelical population[42] and competed for its support by importing special attractions and drafting unusual and sensational ads. The following advertising caption reveals something of the lengths to which sectarian preachers occasionally descended: "Come and sit under the spout, where the glory comes out."

Except for Divine Science, the newspaper advertising of the cults was formal and dignified like that of the denominations. Miss Chew's advertisements, however, were unconventional in that they promised success and personality development in strong, positive terms, as did New Thought advertising elsewhere on the continent.[43] The large number of visitors at Miss Chew's meetings in 1947 indicated that this advertising was not ineffective.

The widespread distribution of literature was another device by which both sects and cults attempted to evangelize the people of Alberta. Nearly all the leading sects, including the Pentecostal Assemblies of Canada, the Nazarenes, the Alliance, the Prairie Bible Institute, the Calgary Prophetic Baptist Institute, and the Disciples of Christ, published their own magazines, either in Alberta or elsewhere in the prairies. Many of these periodicals had a provincial circulation of several thousand copies. The Pentecostal Assemblies of Canada, the Alliance, and the Nazarenes also regularly sold many copies of eastern Canadian or American magazines which propagated their own brand of fundamentalism. The literature fell mainly into the hands of the converted, except for the Prairie Bible Institute's

[40]The writer was informed by a prominent member of the Edmonton Christian Missionary Alliance that at a typical evening service held in the Dreamland Theatre—when the pastor was the Rev. J. D. Carlson of radio fame—an attempt was made to determine the religious leaning of the crowd by a show of hands. It was noted that of the 750 persons at this service, only about 80 were members of the Christian Missionary Alliance. Almost as many again confessed to being Pentecostals. About 30 per cent claimed no church affiliation.

[41]Cf. C. Seidenspenner, "Religion on the Bandwagon," The Christian Century (Chicago, Ill.), Sept. 24, 1947, p. 1142.

[42]Apparently many ordinary evangelicals tended to be religiously footloose. A leader in Edmonton evangelical circles confessed to the writer: "Getting steady church members is a constant problem. . . . It always seems hard to build up a large church membership among evangelicals. They are always drifting off to hear another evangelist."

[43]Cf. L. S. Reed, The Healing Cults (Chicago, 1932), pp. 87–8.

Prairie Overcomer and the Calgary Prophetic Baptist Institute's *Prophetic Voice,* each of which was printed locally and mailed free to a list of over 5,000 friends and sympathizers; both these periodicals may be considered radio follow-up devices which served to reinforce the influence of the group's regular broadcasts among converted and unconverted alike.

It was the two millenial sects, the Seventh Day Adventists and the Jehovah's Witnesses, which made the most effective use of literature. They pioneered in the buying and operating of extensive printing establishments devoted solely to the publication of religious material. The Seventh Day Adventists had a printing plant at Oshawa which began turning out large amounts of religious literature in the early twenties, some of it in various European languages.[44] After the First World War, Adventist supporters and full-time colporteurs, some of whom spoke German and Ukrainian, distributed this literature throughout Alberta. Minutes of the Western Baptist Union for 1921 indicate the effectiveness of this technique of evangelization: "All the bodies mentioned above [the Seventh Day Adventists, Russellites, Pentecostals and Social Revolutionaries] are flooding the people with their literature and much harm is done to the unwary and undiscerning who are easily carried away by such propaganda in the absence of anything to counter it." In 1944, total literature sales in Canada for a ten-month period reached the sum of $425,000; the year 1945 marked "the beginning of a five-year Dominion-wide literature distribution program to reach every home in Canada and Newfoundland."[45]

From its earliest days, the Jehovah's Witness organization concentrated heavily upon evangelism through the printed word. By owning its own plant, buying supplies in large quantities, and hiring only members as workers—at $10 a month plus board and room—it turned out books and magazines at a low cost. Members paid 5c for pamphlets and 20c for books and sold them at whatever they could get, pocketing any profit, and absorbing any loss. Thus, a great variety of religious literature was brought to the public at prices almost anyone could pay. In the beginning, although every conscientious member was expected to distribute literature regularly, much of the selling was done by full-time workers called, after 1934, Pioneers. Both the full-time workers and the ordinary members concentrated upon door-to-door canvassing,

---

[44]Cf. C. B. Haynes, *The Seventh Day Adventists, Their Work and Teachings* (Oshawa, 1935), pp. 92–4.
[45]*Review and Sabbath Herald,* Jan. 3, 1946, p. 19.

for the Society believed this method "succeeded not only in distributing the literature most efficiently but also in attracting the greatest number of converts."[46] In the late thirties every active member of the sect was enrolled as a "publisher" and required to spend at least ten hours a week distributing literature on street corners or from door-to-door. In 1940, there were more than 500 publishers in Alberta, in addition to a number of Pioneers. By 1946, over 1,000 publishers were working in the province. Door-to-door canvassing brought great numbers of people into personal contact with zealous representatives of the sect. The Witnesses' practice of trying for a return or "back" call during which they promoted their convictions with dogmatic zeal, wherever there was the slightest show of interest, often led to conversions. Door-to-door sale of literature was particularly designed to win support from rural dwellers, who had more free time for reading in the winter months than city dwellers with their busy leisure-time programmes, and who were generally less critical of the contents of books and magazines, tending to believe that anything in print "must be true," especially if backed by scriptural arguments. In outlying prairie communities, where it was not uncommon to find people who studied the Bible with great care, Witness propaganda and its bibliolatry often brought a favourable response. This was particularly true of German and Ukrainian settlers who found that the Witness salesmen had literature in their own language; the lack of acquaintance with the Bible of many Roman Catholic and orthodox adherents facilitated acceptance by such people of the Witnesses' peculiarities of exegesis. A report concerning replies to a questionnaire sent out in 1926 by the Alberta Home Mission Committee of the United Church indicates the extent and efficiency of Witness literature distribution at this early date:

It is in the rural parts where these fanatic beliefs secure a foothold and that by various means (radio, preaching, free literature). The International Bible Students' Association is now publishing its interpretation of Christianity in the Ukrainian language. . . . Some localities are much affected by one or other of these "isms." One of our foreign missionaries who spent several weeks in the rural parts of the province this winter declares that Russellism has a strong hold. Another declares that Russellism literature may be found in 75% of his homes.[47]

Evangelism by literature was fundamental to the expansion of the two main adventist sects. Since they lacked an emotional, attractive form of service, great orators, or radio evangelists, this became their key propaganda method. The comparative weakness of the two other

[46]H. H. Stroup, *The Jehovah's Witnesses* (New York, 1945), pp. 56–7.
[47]*Minutes of the Alberta Conference of the United Church of Canada*, 1927, Report of the Home Mission Committee.

millenial sects, the Christadelphians and British Israelites, probably owed much to the fact that neither engaged in extensive literature distribution.

The achievements of adventist sects with religious literature were early recognized by some of the denominations. In 1925, the Union Baptists noted at their prairie-wide conference: "Literature and more literature is a great necessity if we are to contact effectively our distant Baptists. . . . A competent committee on literature should be appointed and charged with the definite responsibilty of developing this effective instrument of the church."[48] At the 1943 Conference, it was urged that, due to the multiplicity of sects, pamphlets be prepared "setting forth the essential position of such sects and denominations, clearly indicating where error is believed to exist.[49] The United Church passed similar resolutions. The denominations, however, failed to grasp fully the opportunities for literature evangelism that existed within an agrarian society like Alberta, with its long winter slack season, nor did they command the cheap printing facilities or the numbers of salesmen that were available to millenial groups. At no time between 1920 and 1946 were they able to produce any quantity of magazines or evangelizing literature of interest to the rural population.

Most of the cults in Alberta employed literature evangelism. Christian Science from its earliest days emphasized the role of magazines and books in the education of its supporters and the making of converts. Mrs. Eddy in 1883 founded the *Christian Science Journal,* in 1899 the *Christian Science Sentinel,* a weekly, and in 1908 the daily newspaper, the *Christian Science Monitor.* The influence of the latter, especially in winning public sympathy for the movement, has been incalculable. In addition, Mrs. Eddy's text book, *Science and Health with Key to the Scriptures,* attained a large sale. To promote the circulation of their newspapers and books, Christian Science erected library-like reading rooms which loaned out literature free of charge. By 1946 there were two of these in Alberta, at Edmonton and Calgary. However, the dignified facades and scholarly atmosphere of these establishments seemed designed more to impress the passer-by with the intellectual status and respectability of the cult than to attract new adherents. In addition, literature racks displaying free copies of the *Sentinel,* the *Journal* and the *Christian Science*

[48]*Minutes of the Baptist Union of Western Canada,* 1925, Report on Literature of the Interprovincial Committee.
[49]*Ibid.,* 1942–3.

Monitor, were placed in railroad stations, hotels, the lobbies of public buildings, and the corridors of high schools. Owing to its intellectual and middle-class bias, however, Christian Science literature evangelism had a limited appeal in Alberta. The cult's failure to expand after 1920 was probably related to its adherence to such conventional and class-limited material.

By contrast, the Unity Truth movement combined a prodigious output of literature with imaginative methods of distribution.[50] Beginning before the First World War with one small magazine called *Unity,* by 1945 the movement was publishing seven different periodicals with a combined monthly circulation of over one million copies. The magazines, many of which were sold on newstands and enjoyed a wide circulation outside of regular Unity followers, included: *Wee Wisdom,* for children, which had over 200,000 subscribers in the early forties; *Good Business,* which specialized in the application of Christian principles to business and "the increase of true prosperity in the world"; *Progress,* a youth magazine; *Daily Word,* which provided inspirational and devotional readings for each day of the month; the Unity Sunday School leaflet, and the two official magazines *Unity* and *Weekly Unity,* in which the teachings of the movement were systematically elaborated. These publications all enjoyed growing popularity in Alberta after 1930. In addition, the Kansas City plant produced many pamphlets with such titles as *Demonstrating Prosperity; Curing Colds through Forgiveness; Casting out Our Demons; Dreams and Their Interpretations; Health through Body Renewal; Obtaining Immortality; Are You Getting All You Want from Life?* New books were also turned out in large numbers at low prices.[51] The total output of Unity publications, including books, booklets, tracts, and so forth ran into several millions. A considerable quantity of this material found its way into Alberta during the thirties and forties.

A special Unity device was the "Prosperity Bank" which resembled a conventional church mite box. As the user put a coin into the box he was to repeat, "God is in charge of all my affairs and abundant good is manifested to me daily." This "affirmation" was supposed to bring prosperity to the user. When the box was full, the money was sent to Unity headquarters in Kansas City for some department of its work. Mr. Lowell Fillmore, a Unity leader, said that at one time

[50]Cf. C. W. Ferguson, *The Confusion of Tongues* (New York, 1928), pp. 210–20; *Unity's Fifty Golden Years,* p. 279.
[51]Volumes recommended for beginners: *Lessons in Truth* by H. Emily Cady, *New Ways to Solve Old Problems* by Lowell Fillmore, and *Working with God* by Gardener Hunting.

13,000 requests for the banks were received monthly, and added "the financial reports on these banks are very gratifying."[52] The boxes, distributed most extensively during the depression, were popular with hard-hit settlers in southern Alberta and helped to attract some of these people into the cult.

Unity's success with literature resulted as much from its novel techniques of distribution and circulation as from the variety and attractiveness of its publications. Like Christian Science, Unity displayed tracts and magazines in jails and hospitals, army and navy centres, industrial homes, and public libraries. Also, in Calgary and Edmonton some of the periodicals were sold at public newstands. Use of the mails was, however, the unique feature of Unity's literature evangelism. In 1909, the leaders organized a correspondence course in Unity principles which in two years had attracted 2,000 subscribers. By the forties, thousands who lived outside the United States had enrolled in the course.[53] A big mail-order business in Unity literature also developed. In 1930, parcel-post and magazine orders reached 1,500 people in Alberta and by 1949 this figure had grown to over 3,000.[54] Another mailing department was Silent Unity which received weekly "on the average of at least 10,000 letters, telegrams and telephone calls from outside the city of Kansas,"[55] and in 1929 brought in goodwill offerings averaging about $1,000 daily.[56] The extent to which this department rendered service to Albertans could not be ascertained. However, Unity's varied and enormous mail-order distribution of literature reached many parts of Alberta and provided the foundation for the organization of congregations in Calgary and Edmonton and the beginning of numerous small home "metaphysical" circles. Without its huge presses and its mail-order system, Unity in 1946 might still have been an insignificant movement.

New Thought groups displayed a good deal of Unity material at their meeting places and they also published and distributed large amounts of their own literature. The Church of Truth and the Church of Divine Science in Alberta benefited by the newsstand sale of such magazines as O. S. Marden's *Success*, Elizabeth Towne's *Nautilus*, and

[52]C. S. Braden, *These Also Believe* (New York, 1949), p. 176.

[53]*Unity's Fifty Golden Years*, p. 65.

[54]From letters to the writer, July 14, 1947, and Aug. 4, 1949, signed by Lowell Fillmore. Unity headquarters indicated that 11,800 Canadians received their literature in 1925, 15,300 in 1930, 19,500 in 1940 and 32,200 in 1946.

[55]Braden, *These Also Believe*, p. 144.

[56]J. W. Teener, "Unity School of Christianity" (Ph.D. Thesis, Chicago, 1939), p. 7.

7

the periodical called *Science of Mind,* as well as by a wide variety of
New Thought pamphlets and books, promising health, wealth and happiness.[57] A few New Thought books, like Ralph Waldo Trine's *In
Tune with the Infinite,* O. S. Marden's *The Victorious Life* and *Be
Good to Yourself,* attained a wide sale on this continent; Trine's book
sold over a million copies. Besides being available through the mail,
many of these books and New Thought magazines were obtainable in
bookstores. Up to 1946, however, few stores in Alberta carried this
material.

The characteristic New Thought mode of literature evangelism
was the cheap correspondence course in metaphysical ideas offered
by a metaphysical college. Varying in content, length, and cost, the
courses aimed at making New Thought doctrines relevant to personality problems of the middle classes.[58] They attracted numerous young
people who sought personality development, social poise, and a
special kind of religious status in New Thought groups. In Alberta,
they apparently aided the growth of the Church of Truth in particular.

Among the occult cults, the Rosicrucians, I Am, and Consumers'
Movement relied heavily upon printed material to disseminate their
doctrines. The Rosicrucians, like Unity Truth, printed pamphlets and
books in their own establishments and mailed them far and wide
to members and inquirers. I Am expansion was linked to the printing and distribution of a large number of pamphlets and books written
by Guy Ballard and published inexpensively by the St. Germain
Press, in California. The books were advertised extensively in American
pulp magazines and until 1940 were distributed largely through the

[57]Some of those advertised in the New Thought Conference prospectus for
1948 included, *Fear Not, How To Change Other People, Mentals and Environmentals,* and *Soul Therapy.*

[58]See W. E. Garrison, *The March of Faith* (New York, 1933), p. 280; Reed,
The Healing Cults, pp. 88–9. The following advertisement from the Church of
Truth's *Fountain* represents the kind of course this cult generally offered:

"University of Metaphysics Home Study Course 'The Fine Art of Living,'
Erma W. Wells.

"This course is designed to help you find your self. There is a way to a life of
peace, joy, health and general well-being. There is a way to know God clearly and
definitely.

"The injunction of old, 'This is the way, walk ye in it' holds for today.

"This Home Study course of 12 lessons shows you how to live, work and play
successfully day by day. Each lesson comes as a printed booklet, pocket size,
so that it can be carried in purse or pocket and studied along the way. At its
successful completion, the student is given full credit towards a degree.

"The suggested offering for the course is ten dollars. Write Home Study
Course, West 1124 Sixth Avenue, Spokane 9, Washington." *Fountain* (Spokane,
Wash.), Aug. 1945.

mails. The beginner's volume, *Unveiled Mysteries* "achieved a remarkable circulation."[59] The I Am required neophytes to read this book and also the second in the series, *The Magic Presence*, before being enrolled in the introductory study group where they were drilled in I Am principles and prepared for membership. After 1940, when the United States government denied the cult normal mailing privileges, the rapid growth of the movement in Alberta was cut short, and only after 1945, when a new policy of lending literature was fully instituted, were slight gains made.

The growth of the Consumers' Movement was intimately associated with the distribution in particular of the *Canadian Consumer*. Although the magazine carried a $2.00 annual subscription rate, most copies were delivered free of charge to householders in selected areas of Winnipeg, Regina, Saskatoon, and Calgary. Some 20,000 copies were circulated monthly, and thus advertisers were guaranteed a sizable reading public. Gratuitous distribution was made possible by the large number of advertisements collected by cult members and by agents, which filled literally half of the space in the magazine. Wherever the magazine aroused sufficient interest, the agents organized study circles or "congregations" which met regularly to discuss printed doctrinal outlines mailed from the cult's headquarters in Winnipeg. Printed material was therefore essential to the very existence of this cult.

As the invention of the radio favoured sectarian advance, so technological developments in newsprint and printing were basic to cult growth. In fact, the expansion of practically all the cult groups was as dependent upon modern, large-scale printing facilities as the Reformation of the sixteenth century was dependent upon the original printings of the Christian scriptures in the vernacular; without diesel printing machines, extensive publishing of cult tracts and books at attractively low prices would have been impossible. Ingenious business-like methods of literature circulation and distribution were no less important;[60] cult groups readily adapted business techniques of advertising and promotion to achieve efficient circulation of their printed literature. The neglect of cheap religious literature pitched to the level of quasi-educated groups by the denominations had left this field wide open.

The cults' use of printed material facilitated expansion into widely scattered towns and cities, while the centralization of writing and

[59]Braden, *These Also Believe*, p. 263.
[60]Cf. M. Bach, *Report to Protestants* (New York, 1948), pp. 185–6.

printing activities in the hands of a few cult leaders guaranteed uniformity of teaching. Local congregations could spring up wherever one or two persons who had read something on the cult offered themselves as organizers. Through their own initiative and with nothing more than a list of other literature-takers in the same area, they were often able to establish a local branch at practically no expense to headquarters. Relations between the central office and the local organizer were inclined to be formal and impersonal, especially at the beginning, and the local leader assumed a role like that of a branch manager of a large business concern. Moreover, the cult use of literature accorded with the contemporary trend toward the individualization of religious belief. The breakdown of conventional religious attachments which accompanied rapid social change after 1914, especially in urban centres, produced growing numbers of people eager to study unconventional theories. Cultist literature capitalized upon the intellectual interests of these people.

The expansion of Alberta's urban centres after 1910 led to new kinds of social developments in the province to which fundamentalist groups addressed themselves with considerable effectiveness. During the period 1912–16, Calgary and Edmonton mushroomed into cities of 60,000 people, and by the early twenties there had appeared in both cities lower working-class and small slum-like interstitial areas. These areas were cut off from the ministrations of the denominations which generally located their church buildings in the downtown and better residential areas and confined their interest to people living in these neighbourhoods. Throughout the period 1910 to 1946, the response of fundamentalist groups to the emergence of these two areas was individualistic and undirected. Evangelical activities were carried on by free-lance preachers who established independent missions in converted stores or other types of buildings; shabby outside and drab inside like the surrounding structures, these buildings usually had but one main room whose seating capacity seldom exceeded sixty people.[61] In Calgary these missions were located in the area bounded by Centre Street on the west, the Bow River on the north, Second Avenue on the south, and Fifth Street on the east, a

[61]The Calvary Mission was described as follows: "The mission is one of an old block of stores. From the outside it presents a very disreputable picture—the landlord does not want the evangelist to make any changes whatsoever and consequently the evangelist has to leave some old and dirty pieces of canvas covering the windows. The inside, however, is quite bright, having been painted by the evangelist just prior to his present landlord's ('no change') decree. The room is about 30' x 50' and seats about 50 people."

district of cheap rooming houses, run-down apartments, and slum-like houses, and noted for a considerable amount of transiency and some prostitution.

A brief sketch of the various missions which sprang up in this section of Calgary will provide a basis for understanding their role and effectiveness in meeting the social needs of such areas. Between 1910 and 1911, the East End Mission and the Calgary Gospel Mission were started, and were joined in 1916 by the "Mission Hall." By 1921, two more such missions had sprung up, the Bethel Mission and the Peoples' Pentecostal Chapel; during the early twenties, two more were opened, the Faith Mission and the Great West Bible Mission. Later in the same period, the Great West Bible Mission and the People's Pentecostal Chapel closed their doors. At this point, the number of evangelical missions showed signs of becoming stabilized, corresponding to the gradual stablization of life then occurring in Calgary. At the same time, the Salvation Army hostel on 9th Avenue increasingly concentrated upon social service activities and finally became a relief centre rather than a genuine mission. Then, with the onset of the depression, two new missions emerged, the Rawson Centre and the Elim Mission. Owing to the severity of economic conditions, the former, along with the two oldest missions, the East End Mission and the Mission Hall, were forced to close in the next few years. In consequence, by 1935 Calgary had only four free-lance fundamentalist evangelists. During the war years increasing prosperity and growing fundamentalist strength added three more groups to this number, namely the Burning Bush Mission, the Lighthouse Mission, and the Calvary Mission; by 1946, however, three institutions, the Elim, the Burning Bush, and Bethel Missions had ceased operating.

Fluctuation in the number of Calgary's missions reflected social conditions within the interstitial areas. Periods of peak development during the years 1930–32 and 1940–43 occurred at precisely the time when Calgary was receiving an unusual number of migrants, many of whom poured into this particular area. The increased number of missions was a response to the greater population and intensified instability of the district. Later, as social conditions improved, some missions were less urgently needed and collapsed. The transiency of these institutions was also affected by other factors, such as competition for support, financial difficulties, the instability of leadership imported into the area from outside, and residential mobility within the area served. The independent character of these evangelical missions with their consequent lack of institutionalized financial support made their financial position constantly precarious. Even success in winning converts failed to guarantee a mission's permanency, since most authentic converts—the number of backsliders was high—rose up the economic ladder, moved out of the area, and then joined a permanent sectarian congregation. Mrs. McKillop of the Calgary Gospel Mission stated that "people saved by the mission are soon lost to uptown churches, because the latter provide a better church home." Other mission leaders made similar statements. The instability of evangelical missions represented the almost inevitable adjustment of these institutions to an area itself highly unstable; their impermanent character was an accommodation to the social instabilities of a transitional area.

In addition to feeding converts to regular sectarian congregations, institutions like the Calgary Mission which specialized in Sunday school activity[62] laid the foundations among working-class children for interest in fundamentalism in later life. Other missions by engaging in welfare activities built up goodwill for evangelical sects among the unemployed and destitute. Although never large nor flourishing, the free-lance missions did constitute a reasonably effective technique of evangelism within the interstitial areas, the value of which was enhanced by the almost complete neglect of these areas by the denominational churches.[63]

Certain fundamentalist sects also penetrated the interstitial area through regular street-corner meetings. Up to the mid-twenties, the "Army" had done this with considerable effectiveness in Calgary and Edmonton, but later their street services became formal and stereotyped and some of the younger sects forged ahead in the use of street meetings. In Calgary, the Pentecostal Assemblies of Canada, the Apostolic Church of Pentecost, the Calgary Prophetic and Regular Baptists, and the Salvation Army held weekly services in the summer of 1946. The regular "stands" used by the various groups were within one or two blocks of the railway station, on the edge of the interstitial area, and thus within easy hearing distance of many of the area's footloose and lonely inhabitants. During the depression the meetings

[62]This Mission during the fall and winter carried on activities almost every night for the children. Mr. Leonard, the evangelist, also had a Saturday morning radio broadcast in which he and several of the children took part.

[63]The short-lived Manson Centre of the Anglican Church, which confined itself to relief functions, was the only recorded denominational effort, apart from depression food lines.

were effective in attracting people to the sect's Sunday services, but by the early forties they did not draw many listeners[64] or assist significantly in building up urban sect congregations.

During the late thirties and the forties, the Jehovah's Witnesses used several ingenious methods of evangelism in the downtown and interstitial areas of Calgary and Edmonton. These included sandwich board advertising, literature vending on street corners, and sound truck advertising of important public meetings. On certain occasions, the three techniques were employed simultaneously to attract the attention of the curious and the religiously unattached. The number of Witnesses who commonly took part in such work of evangelism impressed people with the growth and success of the sect and strengthened its appeal.

After 1940, the fundamentalist movement in Alberta was strengthened by the opening up of missions in the suburbs of Calgary and Edmonton. A Sunday school was usually organized first, and later a congregation. By 1946, either specific sects or non-denominational committees of sectarians had set up at least one Sunday school in every important suburban area of Calgary. In the extreme east end, there was the professedly non-denominational Inglewood (Firehall) Mission, organized in the early twenties and operating a sizable Sunday school with help from the Calgary Prophetic Baptist Church. On the southeast there was the co-operating Bonnyfield Gospel Mission, organized in 1943, and supported by fundamentalist Baptists. On the extreme west, the Plymouth Brethren had a Sunday school at Critchley near Bowness Park. In southwest Calgary, the Disciples of Christ held a Sunday school in the local school building. On the south side at Parkhill they had also opened a Sunday school in 1944 using a former United Church building. Not far away, there emerged about the same time an independent evangelical institutional called the Manchester Gospel Mission which concentrated largely upon the children although it did have a small adult congregation. In 1947, it was operated by a recent graduate of Briercrest Bible Institute. In South Calgary there was also an evangelical Sunday school at Ogden run by a Plymouth Brethren layman and one at Valleyfield run by a Pentecostal. By 1946, the combined attendance at these suburban Sunday schools was in the neighbourhood of 450 children.[65]

---

[64]On one Saturday, in Sept. 1946, the audience included only ten people, although it would often be larger than this number.

[65]Attendance at these missions was as follows: Idlewood, 175; Parkhill, 80; Manchester, 30; Ogden, 25; Bonnyfield, 35; Critchley, 50; and Valleyfield, 30.

By beginning with a Sunday school, the sects found it possible to draw in numbers of children whose parents were indifferent to church-going but felt obliged to send their offspring to a Sunday school. A non-sectarian school was frequently welcomed where a sectarian Sunday school would have encountered resistance. Intense evangelistic indocrination not only accustomed the scholars to fundamentalist symbols and sentiment, but occasionally exerted a considerable influence upon parents. By holding a Sunday school class for adults or an adult service, it was possible to draw in older people and develop rudimentary congregations of fifteen to twenty-five persons. The almost complete neglect of the newer suburbs by the denominations[66] meant that these areas were left dependent upon the services of the fundamentalist sects.

The success of the Disciples of Christ in the Tuxedo district of North Calgary illustrates sectarian initiative in one suburban area. In the first years of the depression, a Disciples pastor began work in Tuxedo, concentrating on a non-denominational Sunday school. The United Church, having been forced by a shortage of ministers to withdraw from the district, was persuaded to make its building available. In 1939, the Sunday school and congregation outgrew this building, and built their own. By 1946, there was a Sunday school of 175 pupils and a congregation of 160. The size of their following was generally not duplicated in other suburban sect ventures in Alberta but it did indicate the possibilities of sectarian initiative in a well-populated, labouring-class suburb.

The non-denominational Child for Christ Crusade of the early forties was another device for evangelizing working-class people in Calgary and Edmonton. The Crusade enlisted Bible school students and other fundamentalists to teach evangelical doctrine to children of school age on Friday afternoons. The meetings were generally held in homes in the better working-class areas. In each city there was a paid secretary, usually a Three Hills graduate, who recruited the teachers and organized the home groups. By meeting on a week-day afternoon, these religious classes drew in many children whose parents belonged to the regular churches. In 1946 this organization had nearly forty home Sunday schools in Calgary and Edmonton with a combined enrolment of more than five hundred children. Some of these children received denominational religious instruction on Sundays; many others got their only Christian teaching at these "home" meetings. By means of this programme of informal religious instruc-

[66]The only major exception in Calgary in 1946 was the Anglican mission in Bowness.

tion, the sects not only increased the number of children brought under their influence, but also impressed some parents with their zeal and drew them into the fundamentalist movement.

Two other inter-denominational evangelical associations which strengthened the fundamentalist movement in Alberta after 1940 were the Varsity Christian Fellowship and the Youth for Christ organization. The former worked among students at high school and university; the latter held regular revival rallies for youth of all types. By 1946, the provincial secretary of the Varsity Christian Fellowship had organized study groups in the high schools of Calgary, Edmonton, Red Deer, and Drumheller, which met in the school at noon hour or after four to study the Bible and foreign missions. Calgary had six such groups in 1946 with a total membership of approximately 80. There was a comparable number in Edmonton. In addition, the Varsity Christian Fellowship had a considerable following at the University of Alberta. Through its study groups and special evangelistic meetings, the organization held together fundamentalist-minded youth in high school and college and also drew into their ranks some young people of denominational background. The emphasis which it laid upon foreign missionary work and the value of Bible school training strengthened these two aspects of the fundamentalist cause, and its total programme helped to train youth for leadership in various sects and to foster inter-sectarian co-operation.

Youth for Christ activity was initiated by co-operating committees of prominent evangelical pastors in Calgary, Edmonton, and some of the smaller cities. The most active leaders were usually the pastors of the Pentecostal Assemblies of Canada, the Nazarene Church, the "Alliance," the Apostolic Church of Pentecost, and the fundamentalist Baptist groups. Youth for Christ rallies were "jazzed up" religious meetings with peppy hymn singing, special musical talent, movies, and outstanding evangelists, many of whom were flown in from the United States. Saturday night rallies in Calgary and Edmonton, usually held in a high school auditorium, often drew over a thousand persons. Fewer than 70 per cent of these were people under thirty years of age; the balance were older persons of evangelical background who attended simply because they enjoyed such revival-like gatherings. The meetings failed to win many converts to the sects. For instance, though 225 persons professed conversion at the fall and winter meetings of 1945 in Calgary, many of these were either "backsliders" or young people already participating in some way in a fundamentalist group. Some were nominal members of the United or Anglican churches, but few of these were drawn into a permanent connection with a particular fundamentalist group. On the other hand, the movement did serve to strengthen many fundamentalist youth in their beliefs and provided Saturday evening recreation for young people who did not dance or go to movies.

A technique of evangelism reminiscent of frontier camp meetings was employed in Alberta's cities after the First World War with considerable profit to the fundamentalist cause. This was the mass revival meeting of the "bandwagon religion" variety, in which all the time-honoured devices of melodramatic preaching, gospel hymn singing, pentecostal "spirit possession," and faith healing were blended with modern "smart alec" repartee and orchestral music.[67] The evangelists who staged the most successful revival rallies in Edmonton and Calgary were mainly from across the border. Owing to its nearness to the United States, Calgary entertained more of these travelling revivalists than Edmonton. They included Dr. C. S. Price of California, who visited Calgary twice in the twenties and again late in the thirties, Aimie Semple MacPherson, Dr. Fuller, California radio evangelist, and a Southern faith healer named William Branham. These evangelists usually came for an entire week and held their meetings in the Calgary Arena, which seats well over 2,000 persons. Dr. Price's appearance early in 1920 or 1921 drew a packed arena for two weeks; Branham preached and healed twice a day for eight days in 1947 and seats in the arena were always at a premium.

The audiences at these rallies usually included large numbers of farmers and villagers from Calgary's hinterland, as well as people from the city itself.[68] Religiously they embraced a large proportion of convinced fundamentalists, some evangelical floaters, and some curiosity-seekers from the denominations. Under the excitement and tension generated by the evangelists, many people responded to appeals for conversion or rededication.[69]Dr. Price's campaigns in the

[67]Cf. C. Seidenspinner, "Religion on the Bandwagon," *Christian Century*, Sept. 24, 1947, p. 1141.

[68]At a Sunday meeting of the Branham healing rally the evangelist asked all those from out of town to raise their hands. At least 50 per cent indicated that they were not residents of Calgary.

[69]Mrs. Thelma Argue, wife of the great Pentecostal leader of Winnipeg, wrote in a private letter, Nov. 30, 1943, concerning bandwagon religion: "We have had 'ex-cowboy evangelists,' 'ex-puglist evangelists,' 'child evangelists,' women evangelists, etc., etc. . . . .While some have considered this humorous, yet the actual fact is the merely breaking routine, merely getting out of the regular course of events; has in itself attracted attention and each one (if a real ministry and call from God was within the heart) has appealed to certain people that perhaps would not have been reached otherwise. . . . As a group becomes well established there may be less room for individual ministries, which may have advantages from one angle (may in fact be necessary) yet lose (in color, intensity of appeal, etc.) when individual initiative becomes lessened."

early twenties[70] were apparently the most influential in this respect. Some six hundred of his converts decided to meet together weekly after he left, but later split up over doctrinal questions into smaller groups. They ultimately contributed to the organization of six new evangelical bodies in Calgary, most of which sprang up without imported leaders or organizers. A considerable number of Dr. Price's converts maintained their sectarian faith, although many did shift from one sect to another. In the late thirties and forties urban revivals were less influential although they usually did give to the sponsoring sect fresh vigour and produced a number of new converts.[71] Denominational abstention from mass revivalism after 1920 facilitated sectarian success with this method.

Many of the techniques adopted by Alberta's fundamentalist groups in the evangelization of the urban centres displayed a significant flexibility of method and an awareness of social needs. Slum missions, street-corner preaching, Sunday schools in peripheral areas, special groups for public school, high school, and college students and bandwagon revivals for the uneducated masses constituted an array of evangelistic methods which revealed at once a marked capacity to improvise and a genuine sensitivity to social and religious needs among important sectors of the urban working class. In almost every case, these techniques, although rarely very original, were intelligently adapted to definite needs of individual groups. Many of the fundamentalist leaders had experience and social connections with the urban labouring class which enabled them to understand the needs of its various sub-groups. A similar awareness was uncommon among denominational leaders whose social outlook and professionalized approach to the ministry tended to preclude a deep understanding of developments in slum and suburban areas, and generally isolated them from many sectors of the working class. Shortages of money and clergy also inhibited denominational activity in certain urban areas.

Certain distinguishing principles stand out in the use of evangelistic media by sects and denominations in Alberta. Both the choice of evangelistic techniques and the way they were employed depended

---

[70]Dr. Price was an exceptionally effective platform evangelist; Pentecostal Assemblies of Canada leaders told the writer that he drew 1,800 for a week to their Sylvan Lake camp meeting in 1943, the largest crowd by far that ever attended the camp.

[71]For instance, the pastor of the Apostolic Church of Pentecost sponsored the Branham faith healing meetings in 1947 to strengthen his congregation and the device apparently worked.

on the ethos and ecclesiastic structure of the religious institution. Thus, methods of the sects were generally influenced, in selection and use, by their typically conservative ethos and by an ecclesiastic structure featuring a non-professionalized type of preacher and a congregational form of polity. Sect conservatism is seen in adherence to old-fashioned methods such as itinerancy, street-corner preaching, and mass revivals. At the same time, the success of much sectarian evangelization, including the work of the Canadian Sunday School Mission, free-lance radio evangelists, missions in urban interstitial areas, and mass urban revivals was related to a congregational form of organization. The independence of the local sect congregation and seminary put individual pastors and Bible school leaders on their mettle, and stimulated both their technique of newspaper advertising and radio broadcasting and specific evangelizing activities in suburban areas and other "fields ripe unto the harvesting." The grass roots character of sect clergy not only facilitated the recruitment of large numbers of young men, making possible extensive itinerancy in rural areas, but it also meant that these men often knew instinctively how to use newspaper advertising and the radio to win a hearing from the lower classes.

With respect to healing cults similar relationships are demonstrable. Christian Science, socially conservative in outlook and highly centralized in organization, confined its evangelizing activities after 1900 principally to dignified "intellectual" literature and public lectures acceptable to the conservative and respectable social classes. Social conservatism was also exemplified by the polished, impeccable exteriors of the reading rooms. The cult's autocratic centralization was visible in various regulations governing the activities of speakers in its Board of Lectureship and prescribing in detail what could pass as official literature. Such rigidities in structure and outlook inhibited adjustment to changing social conditions and were basic factors in the stagnation of this movement in Alberta and elsewhere on the continent after 1920.

The evangelizing methods of other cults were generally geared to their individualistic and business-like ethos[72] and leader-focused type of institutional structure. For instance, the promotional devices of Unity Truth and the Church of Truth were calculated to appeal to lonely, isolated individuals seeking personal adequacy and success and hence included individualized appeals in reading matter of all

[72]Practically all the founders of the healing groups, as well as the I Am, had spent long years in various forms of business activity.

sorts, correspondence courses, "prosperity banks," and daily devotional materials, besides radio addresses on personality development. Their commercial outlook was reflected in a concentration upon inexpensive, easily marketed tracts, magazines, and books, panacea New Thought correspondence courses, and the Silent Unity practice of answering innumerable requests for help and counsel by stereotyped form letter. Few tricks of modern advertising and merchandising were overlooked. The influence of a leader-centred type of structure was visible both in the extent to which the various cult founders dominated organizational policy, including the writing of printed literature as well as the formulating and development of theological beliefs, and in the dependence of local congregations upon the charm and personality of their respective leaders.

The failure of the denominations to match the evangelizing aggressiveness and ingenuity of sectarian and cultist groups in Alberta reflected characteristic features of their ethos and institutional structure. Basically this failure stemmed from a "respectable" middle-class outlook and professionalized "bureaucratic" form of organization. Professionalization of the clergy with its consequent emphasis upon respectability militated against the adoption of "unusual" techniques of advertising, as well as such activities as street-corner preaching and slum missions. The competitive situation militated against individual ministers obtaining regular radio time, except for special, denominationally approved objectives. It also hampered other forms of aggressive evangelism. Seminary education did little to help denominational clergy to broadcast or write religious material of interest to the lower classes. Exigencies of centralization and bureaucratic uniformity retarded denominational utilization of radio and literature evangelism and the opening up of suburban missions. In consequence the denominations registered no significant successes in the fields of radio, literature, itinerancy, or suburban evangelism. Rather, they concentrated, characteristically, upon holding the children and youth through a variegated recreational and social programme and upon maintaining the regular adult congregation. The basic orientation was upon maintenance of the religious status quo. Concern for the neglected sections of the working class was spasmodic and quickly put to one side by the exigencies of preserving the existing congregations with their various goals and organizations. Thus, it was left to newer religious movements to find ways and means of reaching large sections of the working class and certain sections of the urban middle class— and as they met this challenge, they grew in strength and influence.

CHAPTER EIGHT

Conclusion

THIS STUDY of the growth of new sect and cult movements in Alberta has shown the way in which religious organization has adapted itself to changing conditions of social life. The conservatism of the established religious denominations in the face of widespread economic or social dislocations resulting from the nature of the province's development emphasized the advantages of the newer movements of religion with their more flexible organization and techniques. Among important sections of the population the sects and cults replaced the denominations as the predominant forms of religious organization.

The strength of the newer religious bodies was closely related to the loosely integrated character of Alberta's community structure. From its earliest days an unusual set of geographical, socio-economic, and historical forces combined to keep Alberta's community life in a highly unsettled state. Distance from the older cultural centres of eastern Canada weakened the impact of socially organizing institutions and values, while proximity to frontier-like areas in the American Northwest favoured a steady invasion of unorthodox social and religious leaders and associations. The flat, treeless terrain of the southern part of the province early resulted in over-rapid settlement and subsequently in depopulation and community instability. Concentration upon wheat farming in the south aggravated economic instability in a world of fluctuating markets and prices. The province's high variability of temperature and precipitation accentuated the uncertainties of a staple-dominated economy. Both the numbers and range of difference of ethnic and religious groups in the province, none of which held a dominant social position, posed great problems of communal integration. The boom-recession pattern which has been characteristic of Alberta's economic life from the beginning, but the effects of which were most evident in the depression of the 1930's, led to recurring periods of re-settlement and social mobility both in city and country. The Second World War again occasioned large population movements and particularly accentuated the rural-urban drift and the problems of social organization in the cities of Edmonton and Calgary. The result of all these developments was the emergence of an unusually large marginal social element among the population.

The shift in support from the denominations to the sects reflected the way in which these latter bodies met the needs of the marginal sections of the population. In general, while the denominations attempted to serve the interests of established social classes, the sects and cults addressed themselves to the interests of those groups of the population not clearly integrated into the community structure: settlers of European background, farm people compelled in the face of economic conditions and drought to migrate from one part of the province to another, the growing working class thrown up by the rapid expansion of the cities of Calgary and Edmonton. In so far as the new religious movements defended the interests and met the needs of such groups they were assured of substantial support within the Alberta community.

The success achieved by the sects in meeting the social needs of the large European immigrant population in Alberta was clearly evident. The German Baptists, the Evangelical United Brethren, the Swedish Evangelical Mission Covenant, and the World Alliance of Missionary and Evangelical Churches, by integrating numbers of German and Scandinavian immigrants into a religio-social community which preserved their old language and many of their old traditions and customs, served to protect these ethnic groups from social disintegration and to cushion the shock of their adjustment to a new culture. On the other hand, sects like the Pentecostal Assemblies of Canada, the Alliance, and the Prophetic Baptists aided greatly in the ultimate assimilation of people of European background by accepting them on equal terms with Anglo-Saxons.

In the cities, the sects assisted in the adjustment of people of rural background to an urban environment. Their unsophisticated outlook, puritan mores, simple teachings and friendly, informal services made them readily acceptable to persons who had lived a good part of their lives on farms and then moved to the city. In particular, groups like the Pentecostal Assemblies of Canada, the Apostolic Church of Pentecost, and the Church of God assisted in the urban assimilation of the many migrant farmers who poured into Calgary and Edmonton during the twenties and forties. By preserving important rural attitudes and values, the sects softened the impact of the strange urban world upon their members. Urban evangelical expansion may thus be viewed as a stage in the urbanization of rural people with a strong fundamentalist background.

In general, evangelical sects defended basic interests of marginal groups among both the rural and urban lower classes. In the country, they provided a means of social integration to the scattered and lonely, and a socially approved emotionalized "escape" to the economically and socially depressed. In the city, they attracted mainly the un-organized working class, including general labourers, petty clerks, and unskilled factory employees; workers who stood on the margin of the economy and were relatively unprotected from economic disaster. With such groups, the sects emphasized heavenly rewards, religious status, and comradely fellowship and so supplied a partial answer to social inferiority and economic vulnerability. In both urban and rural areas, the sects' interest in newcomers, and their many week-day activities and status-conferring offices, enabled them to draw marginal people into a fairly close-knit socio-religious community. In a province characterized by a high incidence of social marginality, this sectarian function contributed significantly to social integration.

Particular sects tended to meet social needs of specially dislocated groups. Thus sects which emphasized itinerant work reached into the more remote rural areas and furnished religious ministrations where there was an absence of regular denominational services. The Jehovah's Witnesses in particular appealed to the more depressed and backwoods farmers who had profound resentments against city ways and middle-class values. The Witnesses functioned as an important channel for the expression of "backwoods" protest. Their fulminations against commercial interests, militarism, and "corrupted" religion were extreme expressions of hostility and provided an outlet for the intense grievances of certain Anglo-Saxons and new Canadians. Other sects, which levelled a strong polemic against the wealthy modernist churches and staunchly defended traditional puritan and evangelical values, constituted a rallying force for conservative re-ligious groups whose beliefs and way of life had been threatened by extremes of mobility and social change. The fundamentalist attack upon formalism in worship and modernism in doctrine often func-tioned to provide a rationalization for shifts in religious affiliations that, although partly related to theological factors, were mainly the result of the class discrimination implicit in the stiff, unfriendly greet-ings and the middle-class orientation of the services of the denomi-nations. Again, by reiterating biblical authority and old-fashioned Protestant beliefs, sectarian preachers strengthened basic religious symbols and encouraged their listeners to endure the strains of periods of crisis. Homilectical emphasis upon the notion that personal crises and their attendant strains constituted justifiable divine punishment for sin not only furnished lower-class people with a simple, acceptable explanation of their suffering, but occasionally accentuated feelings of guilt and paved the way for the moral reorientation and reorganization of "backsliders." Especially after 1930, the socio-economic situation in Alberta called for institutions to support the traditional values against the impact of urbanism, modernism, and acute social dislocations. This was one prominent function of the evangelical sects.

Aberhart's denunciations of greedy, unscrupulous money-lenders, of eastern financial interests, and of wealthy churches, merit special mention as furnishing an outlet for the grievances of important marginal and economically depressed groups. If utterly suppressed, the deep hostilities of such groups might ultimately have had serious repercussions upon the province's social stability. Aberhart's entry into politics in 1935, apparently motivated by a sincere desire to relieve the lot of the masses, tended to associate fundamentalist religion with basic economic needs of the Alberta population. The charismatic quality of his leadership was also an answer to the social chaos of the depression period and constituted a basic factor in his political success. A great proportion of the fundamentalist movement had come to know and admire Aberhart through his religious broadcasting and were thus favourably disposed to his political adventure. The support given him stemmed partly from basic parallels between his evangelical group and the Social Credit movement. Both were lay rather than professional movements, non-conformist in temper, hostile to the respectable well-to-do and to eastern interests, and both made their strongest appeal to the economically hard-hit sections of the population. Also, both were essentially rural and unpremeditated reactionary protests. Moreover, as a body, fundamentalists were characteristically uninterested and unskilled in political activities and therefore easily swayed by strong hopes and emotions. Distrusting the established parties on moral grounds, they sought a new political deal and an end to destitution and poverty. They considered Aberhart a great religious teacher and leader, uncorrupted by politics or professional clericalism, who was morally unimpeachable, highly gifted in speaking and organizing, and whose interests were identified with those of the masses. In consequence, Aberhart could appeal easily to members of fundamentalist groups, while his radio broadcasting and political activity served to strengthen the evangelical cause throughout Alberta and indirectly helped to weld many of its diverse elements into something of a unified movement.

In the final analysis, the evangelical sects in Alberta carried out a task of social reorganization of considerable importance. Various marginal groups were incorporated into socio-religious communities; the strains of urbanization were cushioned for many rural migrants; grievances were harmlessly channeled off; the needs of the destitute and isolated were partly met; and through the leadership of Mr. Aberhart the province survived one of the most critical economic and political crises it had faced in its history. Sectarian success undercut potentially revolutionary impulses. While the main denominations began to align themselves with the rising middle classes, evangelical sects came to defend some of the interests of the lower-class groups. On the whole, the fundamentalist movement represented a reactionary and decentralizing influence in Alberta's community life. It constituted a reaction against the forces of urbanism, cultural maturity, and centralization both economic and religious, and a defence of past traditions and mores, of the rural against the urban and of the cultural independence of immigrant ethnic groups. Its reactionary and negative attitude to new religious trends and to modern amusements was, apparently, a function of its marginal status and unlettered, strongly rural membership. On the other hand, the very vigour and scope of its protest acted as a corrective to insistent economic forces of urbanization, centralization, and uniformity that tended to twist and uproot deep-lying traditions and symbolic systems. In a period of rapid social change, fundamentalism attempted to freeze certain traditional religious values and meanings within a thoroughly rural ideology and hence defend the province's slowly retreating rural society. Indirectly, it also stimulated the denominations to re-examine theological premises and operational policies with a view to getting closer to the masses. Finally, through its influence upon educational and political developments, the movement played a significant role in preserving the peculiar independence and outlook of Alberta within the larger community structure of Canada.

Compared with the sects, the cults exerted a relatively insignificant influence upon the social life of the province. They never attracted any great number of supporters and their work was almost wholly confined to the two cities of Edmonton and Calgary. Compared with eastern Canada, however, the success of the cults in Alberta was rather striking; Calgary, in particular, seemed to offer a fertile field for their growth. Conditions there which bred the cults could be found in any other Canadian city, but not perhaps to such a marked degree. Isolated from eastern Canada, still "frontier" in much of its outlook, and in close contact with the highly urbanized centres of the Pacific Coast, the society of Calgary exhibited some of the manifestations of extreme urbanism while still lacking many of the social supports of a well-balanced urban social structure. Cultism thus in Alberta reflected in accentuated form the instabilities of urban society. In this way it probably had a social significance much greater than would seem indicated by the small numbers attached to it. Its appeal to people apparently well educated and reasonably well off economically suggests that in certain large areas of our urban society—among that section of the population conventionally thought of as the staid middle class—exist trouble spots only yet slightly explored. This study has done nothing more than offer a hint of the nature and extent of such trouble spots. It does, however, it is hoped, point the way to further fruitful investigations which may be undertaken in this area.

Index

ABERHART, W., 22, 46, 55, 57, 116, 119–22, 124, 129, 134, 156 f.; *see also* Calgary Prophetic Bible Institute
Acadia University, 91
"affirmations," 60–4, 78, 139
Alberta: community structure, 153; legislature, 19
Alberta Bible Academy (Swedish Baptist), 122
Alberta Bible College, 83, 98, 128
Alberta Bible Institute, 83, 128
Alberta School of Religion, 69, 118
All-Canada Baptist Federation, 75
All-Canada Disciples of Christ, 14–15
Alliance, The, *see* Christian and Missionary Alliance
American Order of the Rosy Cross (AMORC), 17, 24
Anastasia, 18
Anglican Church, *see* Church of England in Canada
Anglo-Saxons, 12, 14, 17, 68, 98, 110, 154 f.; as Bible school principals, 90; converts to sects, 34; as cult supporters, 40
Apostolic Church of Pentecost, 20, 30, 33f., 68, 71, 113, 145, 148, 150; doctrine, 52; rural followers, 32, 154
Apostolic Faith Mission, 23, 30, 113
Argue, Mrs. Thelma, 149
Armageddon, 56 f.
Arminian doctrine, 52
Arrowwood (Alta.), 18
Assemblies of God, 19
Association of Gospel Churches, 89, 106
Athabasca, Anglican Diocese of, 48, 117, 129
Atkins, G. G., *Modern Cults and Religious Movements*, 7, 41

BACH, REV. MARCUS, 22, 61, 63, 66, 81, 142

Baden, "Dr.," 26
Ballard, Guy, 25, 61, 141
Ballard, Mrs. Guy, 40
Banff (Alta.), 39
Baptist Union of Western Canada, 27, 29, 31, 33 f., 45 f., 53, 54, 75, 91 ff., 95, 97, 99 f., 107, 117, 119, 123, 138,; loss to sects, 55; radio broadcasting, 129 f.; sermons, 53; services, 51, 67, 70; Minutes of Conference, 70, 91, 93, 97–9, 130, 136, 138
Barrhead (Alta.), 125
Bashaw (Alta.), 113
Battersea (Alta.), 113
Becker, H., 6
Bental, Rev., 87
Berean Bible School, 120
Bethel Bible Institute, 83, 87, 98, 104
Bethel Mission, 144
Bible, The, 15, 27, 38, 43, 52 ff., 57, 62 f., 82, 84, 103, 108, 110, 115, 126, 137, 148; classes, 22, 119; correspondence courses, 114 f., 118 f.
Bible Institute Baptist Church (Aberhart's), 22; *see also* Calgary Prophetic Bible Institute
Bible schools, 74, 82, 96, 104–8, 120 ff., 128; appeal of, 84–8; entrance requirements, 35, 82, 84; graduates, 124, 127; high school departments, 87–8; intersynodical (Lutheran), 77; programme, 84; radio broadcasting procedures, 89; students, 55, 73, 82, 84, 91, 95, 98, 100, 105, 147; teachers, 34, 36, 82, 90, 151; training procedures, 102–3, 148; yearbooks, 34, 84; *see also* Vacation Bible schools
Bible training institutes (United Church), 76
Bonnyfield Gospel Mission, 146
Boston (Mass.), 110

NAZARENES, see Church of the Nazarene
Nearing, Scott, 69
New Canadians, 34, 36, 98; appeal of sects to, 47, 68, 73, 99, 110, 155
New Norway, 113
New Sweden (Alta.), 10
New Thought, 25, 38, 40 f., 79 ff., 111 f., 135, 140 f., 152; movement, 37, 25; prayers, 64 f.; worship service, 58, 60, 79
Newfoundland, 136
Newman, Louise, 59
Non-Anglo-Saxons, 34 ff., 40, 45, 90, 99 f., 10, 115 f.

OGDEN (Calgary), 146
Olds (Alta.), 86
Oliver, B. J., 19
Ontario, 10–11, 16, 77, 114
Ontario and Quebec Baptist Convention, 23
"Open" Plymouth Brethren, 11
Orthodox Church, 33, 36, 47, 56, 91, 110, 137; clergy, 92; liturgy, 48, 51; size, 31
Oshawa (Ont.), 12, 136
Outlook (Sask.), 91, 107

PALLISER HOTEL, Calgary, 22, 123
Pambrun (Sask.), 83
Parkhill (Calgary), 146
Paul, Rev. H., 132
Peace River (district), 4, 20, 48, 95, 105, 109, 113, 118, 125, 127, 128
Peace River Bible Institute, 83, 102, 118
Peel, B. P., 71
Pentecostal Assemblies of Canada, 24, 34, 74, 82 f., 87, 99, 145, 148, 150; development, 19–20; numbers, 30, 71; radio broadcasting, 122, 128; reasons for growth, 55, 113, 134–5, 154; revivals, 68; rural following, 32, 154; urban location, 33; year book, 99
Pentecostal groups, 18, 21, 23, 33 f., 66, 136
Pentecostal Holiness sect, 20, 24, 30, 132
People's Church, 18
People's Pentecostal Chapel, 144
Personal counselling, 80

Peterson, Rev., 90
Phillips, Rev. C. H., 14
Pierson, M. B., 122 f.
Pleasant Valley (Alta.), 10
Plymouth Brethren, 27–30, 34, 68, 74, 146; economic level of members, 36; rural following, 32; urban location, 33; worship services, 45
Polish-Canadians, 115
Pope, L., Millhands and Preachers, 6, 95
Powell, Dr., 29
Prairie Apostolic Bible Institute, 83 f., 90, 98
Prairie Bible Institute, 4, 29, 82 f., 86, 90 f., 98, 101, 104, 105 f., 125, 127 f., 147; attitude to education, 35; factors in growth, 55, 118, 135; High School department, 88; missions, 24, 30, 34, 89; (foreign) 87; Prairie Overcomer, 51, 136; programme, 85; radio broadcasting, 122
Prayer Book (liturgy), 48
Presbyterian Church in Canada, 29, 33 f., 47–8, 50, 53, 67, 69, 74, 76–7, 91 f., 97, 99 f., 107, 117; ministers, 93–4, 95; Minutes of the Alberta Synod, 93, 97, 107, of the Calgary Synod, 100; radio broadcasting, 129 f.; size, 31
Presbyterianism, 51
Price, Dr., 149–50
Prince Arthur (Sask.), 83, 89, 131
Prophetic Bible Institute, 4, 22, 30; church, 22, 57; Prophetic Voice, 23, 136; radio Sunday School, 22; reasons for growth, 55, 57; rural following, 32; urban following, 33; see also Calgary Prophetic Bible Institute; Bible Institute Baptist Church
Protestant denominations, 5, 31, 53, 75; Bible schools, 107–8; churches in Alberta, 31; evangelistic methods, 152; foreign mission work, 87; heritage, 34, 47; literature distribution, 138; losses to sects, 33, 56; ministers, 92, 95–6, 128; non-Anglo-Saxon following, 35; rural following, 32; worship, 51, 69, 155

QU'APPELLE DIOCESE (Anglican Church), 31
Quimby, Phineas B., 37